Existential Counselling and Psychotherapy

SAGE has been part of the global academic community since 1965, supporting high quality research and learning that transforms society and our understanding of individuals, groups and cultures. SAGE is the independent, innovative, natural home for authors, editors and societies who share our commitment and passion for the social sciences.

Find out more at: **www.sagepublications.com**

Existential Counselling and Psychotherapy

Darren Langdridge

Los Angeles | London | New Delhi
Singapore | Washington DC

Los Angeles | London | New Delhi
Singapore | Washington DC

SAGE Publications Ltd
1 Oliver's Yard
55 City Road
London EC1Y 1SP

SAGE Publications Inc.
2455 Teller Road
Thousand Oaks, California 91320

SAGE Publications India Pvt Ltd
B 1/I 1 Mohan Cooperative Industrial Area
Mathura Road
New Delhi 110 044

SAGE Publications Asia-Pacific Pte Ltd
3 Church Street
#10-04 Samsung Hub
Singapore 049483

© Darren Langdridge 2013

First published 2013

Editor: Alice Oven
Assistant editor: Kate Wharton
Production editor: Rachel Burrows
Copyeditor: Solveig Servian
Proofreader: Jill Birch
Indexer: David Rudeforth
Marketing manager: Tamara Navaratnam
Cover design: Francis Kenney
Typeset by: C&M Digitals (P) Ltd, Chennai, India
Printed by MPG Books Group, Bodmin, Cornwall

Library of Congress Control Number: 2011945765

British Library Cataloguing in Publication data

A catalogue record for this book is available from the British Library

MIX
Paper from
responsible sources
FSC
www.fsc.org   FSC® C018575

ISBN 978–1-84920–768–3
ISBN 978–1-84920–769–0 (pbk)

For Ian and Neil, the heart of my being-in-the-world

Contents

Preface

This book emerged out of my sense that there was a need for a book that not only introduces the core of existential counselling and psychotherapy but also seeks to move the discipline forward by engaging with contemporary developments in theory and practice. As both an existential therapist and academic psychologist I have found myself in the curious and, at times, uncomfortable position of spanning two separate disciplines. This multi-disciplinary background informs much of my work, as both a practitioner and academic, and it is represented here also, albeit in often subtle ways. My journey to becoming a psychotherapist has also been intertwined with my academic career and has not been straightforward. I began my therapeutic work, like many do, in a voluntary capacity drawing on basic counselling skills before making the decision to train in psychoanalysis. Whilst the intellectual lure of psychoanalysis was strong I quickly realised that I would always feel that my own beliefs brought me into conflict with even the most progressive of psychoanalytical theory and practice. It was whilst training in psychoanalysis, however, that I first became aware of existential psychotherapy through a one-off session delivered by Emmy van Deurzen and her chapter in Windy Dryden's *Handbook of Individual Therapy* (1996). Emmy's lecture was inspirational but, unlike my other classmates, I resisted the lure of giving up psychoanalysis for this fascinating alternative. I had committed myself to a psychoanalytic training and felt it would be a betrayal to abandon this on the basis of a single lecture. However, a seed had been planted in consciousness and several years later I abandoned my psychoanalytic training and embraced the existential approach instead. I very quickly realised that I had found a home, a home where I could be comfortable intellectually and emotionally.

My work, and therefore this book, may best be represented as part of the British school of existential therapy. The UK has in my view been leading the development of a form of existential therapy that is both true to its roots in existential philosophy whilst also engaged with contemporary ideas and issues. My own work contained in this book and other publications has sought to honour and address just this dimension. There is a real need to recognise, understand and celebrate the fundamental ideas at the heart of existential practice whilst also seeking to advance our mode of practice so that it is more suited to the social world in which we live and work. I believe very strongly that a thorough grounding in existential philosophy is a prerequisite for effective existential therapeutic practice. I also believe passionately that all of us working from this therapeutic perspective must continually strive to engage with contemporary ideas and issues, whether through developments in continental philosophy, critical social theory or our own awareness of the socio-political context in which we live and work. In my own practice I specialise in working with sexual and gender minority clients and it is here that I have become aware of both the value but also limits of existential therapy. Like any therapeutic modality, existential therapy needs to keep apace with the contemporary world into which we are all thrown and reflect this within our own practice. This does not mean jettisoning the past, not at all, but instead requires that we recognise the ways in which we might develop our theory and practice to better meet the needs of our clients and the challenges they face in these late modern times. I hope this book goes someway to achieving this aim.

Acknowledgements

I would like to thank a number of people who have both inspired and supported me through the production of this book. First of all, like so many people within the British school, I owe a debt of gratitude to Emmy van Deurzen and Ernesto Spinelli for their inspirational writing and teaching: their legacy will live on through the lives of all those they have touched. I would also particularly like to thank Mick Cooper, whose own work and supportive criticism has led me to produce an immeasurably better book than I might otherwise have achieved alone. Finally, I want to thank Alice Oven, Rachel Burrows and all the team at SAGE Publications for their support and patience throughout this project, without which this book might never have seen the light of day.

ONE Introduction

CHAPTER AIMS

This chapter aims to:

- provide an initial definition of existential counselling and psychotherapy that makes the essential elements of this particular therapeutic approach clear and understandable;
- address a number of common misconceptions about the existential perspective and in the process further help to define the core of theory and practice;
- historically and theoretically situate existential counselling and psychotherapy in relation to other forms of counselling and psychotherapy.

Existential counselling and psychotherapy can at first glance appear to be a rather mysterious or esoteric therapeutic approach. Indeed, some existential therapists themselves seem to revel in maintaining a myth that it is not desirable or even possible to define this way of working. This is, however, quite untrue. In brief, existential counselling and psychotherapy involves the application of ideas from existential and hermeneutic philosophy to counselling and psychotherapy within a phenomenological methodological framework. That is unlikely to mean much at this stage but my aim in this chapter, and indeed the book as a whole, is to flesh out that definition such that it becomes clear what is (and what is not!) existential counselling and psychotherapy. It is important to note that there are different approaches to existential therapy, and this book is designed to give you an insight into the approach that I practise and which can be located within what is increasingly called 'the British school'. This is an approach that is both classic, in the sense of staying true to the core of existential philosophy, and also progressive, through the way in which there is engagement with contemporary developments in theory and practise. In this chapter I begin by providing more detail to this definition and in the process pointing you ahead to the ensuing chapters, which cover different aspects of this orientation, in theory and practice. Following that, I discuss a number of misconceptions about this approach. Finally, with this particular form of therapy clearly defined and distinguished from others,

I move on to briefly situate the existential approach within the broader historical, cultural and disciplinary context of counselling and psychotherapy.

What is existential therapy?

I began this chapter with a very brief and rather condensed definition of existential therapy and in this section I unpack that definition so I hope you will have a much clearer understanding of what this particular approach to therapy looks like. The best place to start is with the last element of the definition and the idea that we work within 'a phenomenological methodological framework'. Phenomenology is a philosophical tradition that started with the work of Edmund Husserl (1859–1938), who sought to radically reconceptualise the nature of philosophy itself, but more practically it also resulted in a method of inquiry which aims to 'return to the things in their appearing'. That is, the phenomenological method is focussed on rich description of how the world appears to people rather than drawing on theories which move beyond experience itself. So when thinking psychologically we try to stay as close as possible to how things are experienced by people and attempt to understand what the world is actually like for other people, rather than fit people into our existing theories of how we operate. It is all too easy to assume that everyone experiences the world the same way but of course the reality is that we all have a unique perspective on the world, grounded in our history, our lived experience. Where people have radically different life histories (or are from different cultures) this difference is obvious and we may struggle to understand. But even when we do quite easily understand what other people mean when they tell us of their experience there are dangers in listening when we make assumptions about meanings and miss subtle but important distinctions. This may not seem to matter in everyday conversation (though even there it can have important implications) but is vital in counselling and psychotherapy, where the phenomenological heart of the existential method requires that we come as close to seeing the world from the client's perspective as is possible. This is always an approximation, for we can never really walk in another's shoes, but there are a number of techniques within the phenomenological method that are designed to help us understand what others mean as best we can, without prejudice or presupposition and without projecting our own understanding on to them. The next chapter provides much more detail on the phenomenological method, along with real examples of client work to help appreciate the subtle but important way that this approach works to get us close to the lived experience of others.

The phenomenological method is the foundation for all existential counselling and psychotherapy, but there is more to the existential psychotherapeutic perspective than the phenomenological method alone. The second key element, mentioned in the definition above, involves the application of ideas from existential and hermeneutic philosophy to counselling and psychotherapy. Existential counselling and psychotherapy is deeply indebted to philosophy. Indeed, some even consider it to be a philosophical approach to counselling and psychotherapy (see Deurzen and Adams, 2011) as the philosophy of phenomenology provides the method, supplemented by the philosophies of existentialism and hermeneutics in practice.

Existentialism is a school of philosophy associated with such figures as Martin Heidegger (1889–1976) and Jean-Paul Sartre (1905–1980). Philosophers such as these (and others too, who will be discussed in the following chapters) sought to examine the nature of existence itself. Through sustained philosophical argument they focussed attention on the nature of being (*ontology*) and what we can know about existence (*epistemology*). These may appear rather abstract ideas but this stems from the assumptions that most of us have about our own existence, which are grounded in our own particular cultural histories. These philosophers attempted to set aside any such assumptions about existence (putting aside the *natural attitude*, our everyday way of thinking about the world) using the phenomenological method so that they could formulate an understanding of existence that is free from such prejudices. So, for instance, at this time, in the West at least, there is an assumption (as a result of a hundred years of psychological theorising filtering down into popular culture) that people have particular personalities: 'she's really outgoing'; 'he is so shy' and so on. This tendency whilst appearing to describe ourselves and others is more than simple (phenomenological) description, for it brings all sorts of theoretical assumptions to bear on how we understand ourselves and others. Having a personality type implies having a fixed nature or character and suggests that we can predict how someone will react in any given situation. The extrovert is likely to be the life and soul of the party, be confident in strange situations and find it easy to connect with others. The reality of course, as any good observer of human nature will testify, is that people are much more complex than this and much less predictable. The 'so called' extrovert may be painfully shy at some moments or at different times in life. This may be covered up in an attempt to preserve the sense of identity as an extrovert ascribed to them by others, but with close observation the cracks will ultimately show. Conversely, the introvert may demonstrate considerable courage in new situations that surprise all those who thought they knew them. Existential philosophers have provided a valuable corrective to assumptions like the notion of personalities and suggested radically different alternatives for understanding human nature. So, for instance, existentialists do not understand people as fixed personalities but rather as beings that have no fixed core but are always engaged in the process of life, creating new meaning for themselves moment by moment. This subtle but important shift has huge implications for how we understand life and also how we practise counselling and psychotherapy. Without any simple notion of fixed personalities, people have many more possibilities in life to transform themselves, to realise their potential and to become who they want to be rather than who they assume they must be.

Hermeneutic philosophy has an even longer history than existentialism, beginning in the 17th Century with scholars attempting to understand the divine word of God through scripture but now most often associated with philosophers such as Hans Georg Gadamer (1900–2002) and Paul Ricoeur (1913–2005). Their work was concerned with interpretation and how we can understand what is being communicated, principally through text and later still broader forms of discourse, such as speech. What these philosophers realised was that whilst we often seem to grasp meaning relatively easily, there is a process of interpretation involved to bridge the barrier between ourselves and others, whether that other is God (expressed through scripture) or simply another human being that we engage in conversation. Ideas about how we communicate and come to understand others and how they experience the world are, of course, vital to effective psychotherapeutic practice and form another element in existential counselling and psychotherapy. As counsellors and psychotherapists we need to work hard to know our clients, to really understand them and find the bridge between our way of seeing the world and their own, and hermeneutic methods provide an additional tool to better enable us to do this. In Chapter 11 I introduce some of the key ideas of hermeneutic philosophy and discuss how these ideas translate into a practical method to improve our practice as existential counsellors and psychotherapists.

Whilst existential and hermeneutic philosophies (and indeed, phenomenology too) are practical philosophies, principally concerned with the nature of existence and how we can come to understand it, there is still a process of translation needed to take these sophisticated ideas and use them practically and psychotherapeutically with clients. The history of existential counselling and psychotherapy (described in brief below) is a history of the translation and application of philosophical ideas from the existential and hermeneutic traditions into psychotherapeutic practice. Before moving on to provide some brief history, and in the process situate existential counselling and psychotherapy within the broader history of counselling and psychotherapy, I want to first look at and dispel a few of the common myths about existential counselling and psychotherapy.

Common misconceptions

Anything goes?

One of the most pervasive and pernicious myths about existential counselling and psychotherapy is that it is a ragbag 'anything goes' approach to practice. This myth is not without foundation and it is easy to see how it has arisen. Existential counselling and psychotherapy is a psychotherapeutic perspective that avoids technique and emphasises the need for practitioners to find their own ways of working. This distinguishes it from cognitive behavioural therapy (CBT), for instance, where very specific guidance is provided for effective practice and there exists a clear set of techniques which must be utilised. The case for practitioners creating their own form of existential counselling and psychotherapy is, however, rather overstated. Whilst the existential approach is not an approach that might easily be manualised (as we have seen with CBT), this does not mean that we cannot proscribe limits to what is and what is not existential counselling and psychotherapy. There are core principles that underpin the existential approach (described briefly above), and without these there is no existential therapy. Existential counselling and psychotherapy is not an eclectic or integrated form of therapy, which can accommodate ideas from CBT or psychoanalysis, but is instead a philosophically grounded form of therapy with a central core to practice. Trainees and experienced practitioners need to be very cautious when attempting to incorporate ideas from other forms of therapy into their practice, for without a clear philosophical justification there is likely to be confusion for both the therapist and client alike.

All in the head?

Another common misconception about existential counselling and psychotherapy is that it is overly intellectual. It is true that the approach requires a great deal of the therapist intellectually and this is a key criterion for suitability to train as a therapist, but it does not require the same of the client. The role of the therapist is to act as a translator of the often very complex ideas of existential and hermeneutic philosophy and the client need not know anything of the theory which underpins the method. The therapist is the conduit, embodying their knowledge and engaging in a very real manner moment by moment with the client. There are dangers for therapists, of course, in losing sight of the here-and-now experiential element (for instance, around feelings) but that is not an inherent flaw in the approach, as the present is treated seriously by existential philosophers, but rather a result of the need for the therapist to be aware of their own weaknesses. It is likely that people drawn to the existential approach are attracted by the intellectual quality underpinning the method (similar to psychoanalysis), but some of the most eloquent and beautiful existential writing concerns the way in which we are more than simply a mind but rather embodied creatures fundamentally in relation with others. This is not a therapy for those without a heart, for those without passion or for those without care.

Whilst it is important to guard against the dangers of existential therapy being an exercise in academic philosophy, it is also important to avoid the rather overused charge that existential therapists (or perhaps most commonly, trainee existential therapists) are being 'overly intellectual' when engaged in thinking about their client work. It is necessary to engage intellectually with ideas from existentialism and hermeneutics when reflecting on one's client work (for instance, in supervision), for without this we end up with nothing but a watered-down psychoanalysis or person-centred approach to counselling (see below). We must not be afraid of the rich intellectual heritage that underpins our approach and the insights that it may allow into our work with clients.

Isn't that just person-centred counselling?

At its worst existential counselling and psychotherapy can appear to be a rather cold version of person-centred counselling (or conversely, a rather watered-down psychoanalysis), but nothing should be further from the truth. The phenomenological method alone may lead to existential counselling and psychotherapy appearing to cover much of the same ground as person-centred counselling, though without the empathic warmth, but the phenomenological method is just the start and not the end of existential therapy. The core conditions of person-centred counselling of unconditional positive regard and empathic understanding may appear at first glance to be the same as the phenomenological attitude, where we take people's experience seriously and attempt to communicate this back to our clients to enable them to better understand their own situation, but this is not quite right. In particular, there is no essential requirement for empathy in the phenomenological method, though in reality most existential therapists would ensure that rapport is developed early on in the therapeutic relationship, at least in part through some communication of empathy. Similarly, unconditional positive regard is also not key to the phenomenological method, but once again it is likely that good existential therapists will work to develop a warm relationship in the early stages with their clients that is not conditional on any specific criteria. The key differences become more apparent later on in the therapy where an existential therapist is likely to stress the need for the client to take control of their own emotional needs (with less need therefore from the therapist to communicate empathy) and not require high levels of positive regard from the therapist. That is, whilst these core conditions provide the basis for effecting client change in person-centred counselling, they are not understood in the same terms by existential therapists. Existential therapists instead see change occurring in their clients through increased insight and awareness, greater openness to the world (and the choices that may be made) and increased courage and passion to face the inherent difficulties of life, as the result of the combination of the phenomenological method and ideas from existentialism and hermeneutics.

Situating existential counselling and psychotherapy

Existential counselling and psychotherapy has its roots in the work of a number of early psychotherapists, notably Ludwig Binswanger (1881–1966) and Medard Boss (1903–1990). Binswanger and Boss both trained as psychoanalysts who, becoming dissatisfied with this particular theoretical perspective in the 1930s, sought to draw on ideas from existentialism to alter their practice and develop what they referred to as 'Daseinsanalysis'.

This rather ferocious sounding name was inspired by the work of Heidegger who coined the term 'Dasein' to refer to the 'there of being', something which will be explained in Chapter 3 when I discuss his thought in detail. What they did was to keep the psychoanalytic frame (with clients on couches freely recounting anything that concerned them) but stripped away all the psychoanalytic theory and instead focused on staying phenomeno-logically with the client's meaning, drawing on ideas from Heidegger in the most part to offer up therapeutic interventions. This divergence from (mostly Freudian) psychoanalysis was a key moment in the history of exis-tential counselling and psychotherapy. The theoretical assumptions of psy-choanalysis were jettisoned in favour of an approach which took the client's experience seriously, in its own terms. Two of the key psychoanalytic con-cepts which were – and continue to be – rejected by the early existential therapists were the notion of a dynamic unconscious and transference/countertransference. Dream analysis was also central to much early psycho-analytic work though is less central now, but this too was radically re-worked, particularly by Boss (1957), moving it from an analysis of the symbolic to the phenomenological. I discuss this in more detail in Chapter 6. It is worth spending a little time here explaining the existential–phenomenological approach to the unconscious and transference.

The unconscious is a concept, extensively elaborated in psychoanalysis, that warrants particular discussion in the context of existential therapy. Freud did not 'discover' the unconscious as is popularly imagined – the idea had existed long before him in philosophical thought – but he did elaborate and re-vitalise the concept such that it is now part of the wider cultural imagi-nary. Indeed, it is hard to imagine people in the West not thinking in terms of conscious and unconscious aspects of mental life, such is the hold that these ideas have on the public (including many counsellors and psychotherapists). The objection in existential terms is not with things being out of conscious awareness but with the Freudian notion of the unconscious as a repository of all things that are not within consciousness, of treating the unconscious as if it were somewhere in space, a system, rather than a process. The Freudian notion of the unconscious is founded on a causal notion that events in the past are hidden in the unconscious and lead to (or even, determine) how we are in the present. Heidegger's arguments about the multidimensionality of time (see Chapter 3 for more on this), of it being web-like (in Cohn's, 2002, terms) with the past, present and future inextricably linked, suggest that the Freudian conception of the unconscious is mistaken. The idea that feelings being expressed in the present somehow emerge from past events, as a result of being stored in the unconscious, is also a feature of psychoanalysis that does not fit with existential therapy. As Cohn (2002: 121) states:

> existential therapists see feelings as belonging to the situations in which they arise – they can be as little 'detached' from them as the pattern can be detached from the carpet. The anger of today is not the same as the anger of years ago – whatever its relation to the earlier anger may be – it has a new context and is a different anger. The possibility of change depends on the realization that this is so.

The therapeutic relationship within psychoanalysis is also conceptualised differently from that in existential therapy, characterised as it is by a distinction between the real relationship and the transference relationship (later augmented by the complementary idea of countertransference). The result of this tripartite understanding of therapeutic relationship amongst psychoanalysts is a primary focus on transference, the unjustified transferral of feelings from client to therapist. The 'unjustified' element of it is key as it implies that the feelings are not real (that is, left to the adult–adult part of the relationship where the contract and frame is established) but are considered the most important element for effective therapy, where a client can work through previous relationships with the psychoanalytic therapist in the here-and-now of the room and through this gain new insight. For existential therapists all aspects of the relationship between client and therapist are real and require the same approach. The fundamental relatedness of being at the heart of existentialism (see Chapter 8) undercuts any notion of relationships being imagined or fantastical. When engaged phenomenologically with a client we take seriously all aspects of the situation present to us, and that of course includes the relationship between client and therapist. This will undoubtedly be influenced by previous relationships which might need to be elucidated through the phenomenological method, but the relationship that exists between client and therapist is always a real relationship of significance in its own right.

Another parallel development to the work of Boss and Binswanger was that of 'logotherapy', which Viktor Frankl (1905–1997) developed in the late-1920s/early-1930s. Unlike Daseinsanalysis, however, logotherapy rarely employs ideas direct from the existential philosophers but instead draws tangentially on such ideas. Both these approaches continue in a relatively unchanged form today, mostly in Continental Europe. Other key figures in Continental Europe include the psychiatrists Karl Jaspers (1883–1969) and Eugene Minkowski (1885–1972), who both sought to move away from traditional diagnostic categories of mental illness and instead work phenomenologically to understand what such experiences mean for the patient. Their work influenced many others in the existential therapy world, including Ronnie Laing, a key figure in British psychiatry and psychotherapy (see below).

In the US a slightly different take on existential counselling and psychotherapy developed, later in the 1950s, which continues to the present day. This was mainly the result of the influence of Rollo May (1909–1994), a psychologist mentored by the existential philosopher Paul Tillich (1886–1965), who is credited with being 'the father of existential psychology in America' (Hoeller, 1999). Students of May who have become leading figures in the development of existential therapy in the US include James Bugental (1915–2008) and Irving Yalom (1931–). The US version of existential therapy is somewhat different from that most often seen in Europe, with greater links between ideas from humanistic theory (such as the work of Carl Rogers, the founder of person-centred counselling) and less direct use of existential philosophy. Indeed, this is so much the case that American existential therapy is commonly referred to as 'existential-humanistic psychotherapy'. This not only reflects the influence of key figures on the development of this approach but also the American culture, which tends to emphasise the individual and their inherent capacity for growth (an idea central to humanistic theory but not inherent in existentialism).

Existential counselling and psychotherapy in the UK represents one of the most vibrant and continually developing forces in the field. Perhaps the earliest and most significant figure in the development of British existential therapy was Ronnie Laing (1927–1989), a controversial Scottish psychiatrist who brought existential ideas to prominence within psychotherapy in the 1960s. Whilst Laing's influences (and approach to practice) were much broader than existentialism, he sought to offer a radically different understanding of serious mental illness (such as schizophrenia) where the focus was on understanding what was being experienced in the patient's own terms, rather than treating their experience as an illness simply in need of treatment and cure. He emphasised the need to take everyone's experience seriously (as any good phenomenologist might), including those who are traditionally classified as psychotic and normally assumed to be 'too mad' to understand. He also examined possible explanations for severe mental distress and looked primarily towards the family and other relationships for identifying the root cause of such experiences. This social position on mental health and ill-health is the signature in all of Laing's work. No particular school of therapy has followed from Laing, with many followers going on to incorporate the ideas of a wide range of theorists (particularly radical psychoanalytic thinkers such as Lacan) into their theory and practice. His existential legacy is clear, however, in the British school of existential therapy, which still firmly embraces the de-pathologising perspective of Laing (and others, such as Szasz) into their work.

Whilst Laing was the biggest single influence on the early development of British existential therapy, there has been considerable progress from that point. What is now termed 'the British school', which is being represented here in this book, represents one of the most dynamic and cutting-edge approaches to existential therapy anywhere in the world today. There is a relatively pure heart to British existential therapy, with the focus on employing the phenomenological method augmented by ideas from existentialism, but this has not resulted in stagnation (a charge that has been levelled at Daseinsanalysis; see Cooper, 2003) but a continuing interest in working within this spirit to develop practice further, drawing on ideas from thinkers within the same – or closely related – philosophical tradition/s. This combination of an approach that is true to the core of existential therapy together with an openness to new ideas characterises the British school. Two figures central to firmly establishing this tradition are Emmy van Deurzen and Ernesto Spinelli. Their brilliant writing and teaching have inspired the next generation to build on their wisdom to ensure that existential therapy remains a vibrant force within counselling and psychotherapy today and into the future.

The structure of the book

This book is simply structured. Part I on the foundations of theory and practice includes chapters providing detail on the phenomenological method, the development of existential therapy and then the fundamentals of practice. Part II includes five chapters that describe core existential theory and its application to practice, with copious case studies and activities. All of the case studies are based on my work, though none of them simply represent individual people's experiences. In order to preserve anonymity details of the case studies have been substantially altered, with many representing amalgams of different people's stories. The key issues being illustrated, however, are not fictionalised but always based on a real example from my practice. If people recognise the stories being recounted then the case studies will have achieved their aim. Part III includes two chapters designed to advance the theory and practice of existential therapy; this includes a chapter on the importance of research, and the final chapter on power, politics and language where I also briefly discuss my thoughts about the future for this therapeutic perspective. The material in the book will undoubtedly make most sense by reading from start to finish, but it is certainly possible for the more knowledgeable reader to dip in and out of chapters of interest should they wish.

Further reading

Cooper, M. (2003). *Existential therapies*. London: Sage.
An excellent overview of the varieties of existential therapies being practised today.

Langdridge, D. (2010). Existential psychotherapy. In M. Barker, A. Vossler,& D. Langdridge (Eds) *Understanding counselling and psychotherapy*. London: Sage.
A brief introduction to existential therapy with a particular focus on its applicability to working with clients presenting with problems concerning fear and sadness (often understood as anxiety and depression).

Spinelli, E. (2006). *Demystifying therapy*. Ross-on-Wye: PCCS Books.
A broad-based exploration of the assumptions underlying counselling and psychotherapy culminating in Spinelli outlining his own views on the benefits of an existential–phenomenological perspective.

Deurzen, E. van (1996). Existential therapy. In W. Dryden (Ed.) *Handbook of individual therapy*. London: Sage.
A succinct but very clear introduction to what has become known as 'the British school of existential therapy', of which this book is also a part.

Part I

Foundations of Theory and Practice

TWO Introducing Phenomenology

CHAPTER AIMS

This chapter aims to:

- provide detailed information about phenomenological philosophy and how this is employed as a psychotherapeutic method;
- discuss common problems encountered when working phenomenologically in counselling and psychotherapy;
- describe a number of cases demonstrating the value of the phenomenological method for counselling and psychotherapy.

Phenomenology as a strand of philosophy began at the very beginning of the 20th Century with the work of Edmund Husserl. His *Logical Investigations* (published in two parts in 1900 and 1901) represent a clear start to a radical new approach to philosophy. Husserl inspired many important later thinkers, which generated a number of different strands of phenomenological philosophy. The existentialist thought (discussed in detail in the following chapters) of philosophers such as Heidegger, Sartre, Merleau-Ponty and others employs (albeit in quite different ways) the phenomenological methods of Husserl. It is common to hear students (and sometimes teachers) of existential counselling and psychotherapy dismiss Husserl's work rather simplistically as if the developments of thinkers such as Heidegger invalidate what went before. This is a grave mistake, for Husserl's work represents the fundamentals of phenomenology and therefore existential therapeutic practice. This dismissal may be simply the result of an inadequate understanding of the foundations laid by Husserl but may also, I suspect, be the result of a general tendency to believe that new is necessarily better. Wisdom is not the province of what is new in philosophy, therapy or life in general and there is considerable wisdom in Husserl's writing which should not be readily overlooked. In this chapter I draw extensively on Husserl's work to present the fundamentals of phenomenology.

In presenting philosophical theory to people other than philosophers, with their different commitments, it becomes apparent that something must be lost. Philosophy is a discipline of contestation, there is no certainty and no stable foundation and, as such, is a discipline in which the work of philosophers, such as Husserl, is constantly revisited and assessed either in its own terms or in the light of the work of other philosophers, whether they be early

Western philosophers like Aristotle or more recent philosophers like Derrida. This results in a lack of certainty about the meaning of any given text or body of thought, and phenomenology is no exception. There are many different readings of Husserl's writings which if all were considered in this book would result in a treatise on Husserl and his philosophy that is way beyond the needs of most therapists. In the light of this, what I present below (and throughout the book) will be necessarily selective and, at times, a simplification of the philosophical arguments. In effect, I will be engaging in a process of translation, translation of philosophy into methodology (something which is not at odds with Husserl's own agenda and his commitment to producing a new theory of knowledge). I steer a course through the often contested philosophy that I hope will offer enough complexity to allow the reader to understand the heart of phenomenology but not so much that they will be lost in it. My concern is to provide a discussion of the fundamentals necessary for the practice of existential therapy, and not the practice of philosophy itself.

Intentionality

Intentionality is the key concept in phenomenology and represents a radical shift in philosophical thinking from that of previous philosophers but is a concept which is often misunderstood or insufficiently appreciated. 'Intentionality' is a technical term and should not be confused with our every-day understanding of intending, where we might intend to act in a particular way (such as intending to go on a diet or meet with friends). Instead, 'intentionality' refers to the idea that every act of consciousness, every experience we have, is *of something*. That is, every act of consciousness intends something, be it a real object in the world (such as our perception of the therapy room or our client) or something in our memory or imagination (such as our recollections of our childhood or what a client said to us in a previous session). For most people this idea sounds self-evident, rather simplistic and of little consequence, but it is actually crucial for understanding quite why we employ the methods we do when engaged with our clients phenomenologically, in addition to understanding quite why phenomenological philosophy marked such a radical break with the philosophical traditions that went before.

A central problem for philosophers working before Husserl (1900–1901) was something called the 'egocentric predicament'. Indeed, this remains a problem for many philosophers today who have not embraced or been convinced by Husserl's intervention. The egocentric predicament revolves around the idea that if we have minds inside bodies (enclosed as if in some vessel) with thoughts and ideas occurring first and foremost in this enclosure, then how is it possible for such a mind to reach out into the world and engage directly with it? This problem stems from the work of an early philosopher, Rene Descartes (1596–1650), who, in his *Meditations on First Philosophy* (1641/2003), engages in a philosophical process of doubt, of all things about which he cannot be certain and then tries to identify that which can be known for sure. So, he doubts our experience of the world (though not the existence of the world itself) as he believes that this is not given to us directly but is only an idea about which there might be uncertainty. The conclusion of his philosophical enterprise is that it is only possible to know he exists because he is a thinking thing. Everything else can be doubted (setting aside his arguments about God) other than the self-evident fact that as he is the one who is engaged in this particular thinking process then he must exist. The result of this was a distinction between minds (thinking things) and bodies (things extended in the world in space), which is known as 'Cartesian dualism', with the consequent problem of how minds can engage with the world (given that they are not objects extended in the world but rather somehow existing enclosed within bodies), the egocentric predicament.

Husserl's solution to this problem was to provide a radical alternative to the foundations upon which Descartes' work was formed. He argued that things in the world *are* directly given to us in consciousness (they are 'always intended', to use his technical term), rather than being simply ideas or representations of the world, and as such the world is knowable through direct experience and its essence through phenomenological reflection (more on this latter point below). This solves the problem of mind–body dualism, as there is only one kind of stuff (no distinction between minds and bodies), and also the egocentric predicament: we can be certain of things but only as they appear to consciousness.

Biological and cognitive psychology tend to fall foul of the egocentric predicament with their theories of what is going on inside our heads. Scientific understandings such as these have become well known within many (though not all) cultures, and many people accept this position as taken-for-granted knowledge. However, upon reflection the problem (as outlined above) becomes apparent: we know that we go beyond our brains or cognitive processes (internal mental states) but often struggle to make sense of quite how this is achieved. Through the notion of intentionality we realise a world in which our experience is valid, in which we take seriously how the world appears to us and in which the mind is recognised as a public phenomenon. The mind is thus part of the public world, there is no internal or external, no psychological and social (in the traditional sense of those terms).

The final point to make about intentionality is that it is complex and multiple: there is not simply one kind of intentional relation with the world but many. For example, there are perceptual intentions (where we see an object), pictorial intentions (when looking at a painting), intentions of memories and so on ad infinitum. These intentions may be complexly interwoven (as a perceptual intention is required for pictorial intending, you need vision to perceive a painting) and the project of phenomenology proper is to unpick and describe in rich detail all that is intended in the world. The world is used here (and elsewhere in this chapter) to mean the horizon of our experience, that which is available to us, not simply to mean the Universe, Earth or some smaller element therein. The most common objection to Husserl's stance, and one which is important for existential therapists, concerns the possibilities of errors (such as hallucinations and delusions) where things are not as they appear. I may think I have seen a ghost but upon later investigation and reflection recognise that this was simply a shadow projected by a curtain in a darkened room. How can we take intentionality seriously when it can be mistaken? Mistakenly seeing a ghost remains part of the public realm of experience and is still part of my intending and therefore still something that we need to take seriously. I may revise my view about what I have perceived or hold fast to my initial perception, but regardless that is my intention towards my world and must be acknowledged as part of my experience of the world. Existential counsellors and psychotherapists always take the client's experience seriously, whether it appears rational or not, and through this we stay with our clients, respectful of the way the world appears to them in its intending, whilst we seek to understand quite what this means. We do not theorise their experience away or reduce it to prior causes but focus on how it manifests itself in consciousness through the application of the phenomenological method within the therapeutic relationship.

Activity Spend some time reflecting on what it is like or would be like to hear someone speak of something that you do not believe. For instance, if you are sceptical about the existence of ghosts or UFOs, visit some websites where people discuss their experiences of these phenomena. What is it like to hear such stories when you do not believe them personally? Are you able to put your own views to one side and appreciate these are accurate reflections of these people's own beliefs? A crucial element when working as an existential therapist is to work with people's experience as expressed and not impose our own views upon them.

Noema and noesis

Two rather ferocious sounding terms, inherently related to the concept of intentionality, that generate considerable confusion are 'noema' (the object of consciousness) and 'noesis' (the manner in which one is aware of the object of consciousness). They warrant discussion given that they are part of Husserl's phenomenology and further delineate the meaning of intentionality (and indeed are also likely to be mentioned in the phenomenological literature that existential therapists may read) but are highly problematic terms whose meaning is contested within the contemporary phenomenological philosophical literature.

At their simplest, noema refers to the 'what' of experience and noesis the 'how' it is experienced. Noema and noesis should be understood as a correlation and not as separate concepts: they cannot exist apart. They were an attempt by Husserl (1913/1931) to ensure that intentionality was not understood as 'inside' (a person) and always related to something 'outside' (like a real object). Intentionality refers to the way in which consciousness is related to an *immanent* object, an object of awareness to which consciousness is directed, whether this is a real object or something imaginary. Phenomenology must, in Husserl's view, describe both aspects of the noema–noesis correlation, both the 'what' of awareness and 'how' it appears to us. The importance of this correlation is that it emphasises the way in which we must focus on the public realm of experience – what is available to consciousness – rather than engage in a hunt for what is inside the heads of ourselves or others. Of course, this process is predicated on us being creatures with brains and sufficient cognitive capacity to become aware of ourselves (we are conscious), but the focus is not on cognition per se but rather 'the things in their appearing' to consciousness. There are a number of philosophical flaws in this move (see, for example, Bell, 1990), but these need not concern us here with our focus on phenomenology and its implications for therapeutic practice.

For the existential therapist we can, therefore, turn our attention to the 'what' (noematic correlate) of a client's experience and the 'how' (noetic correlate) of it also. Phenomenology is a descriptive enterprise and as existential therapists we keep our focus on description rather than explanation. If we explain something we risk reducing the 'what' and 'how' of their current experience to something supposedly more fundamental (such as past experiences), losing all the detail about their experience as expressed now. We also risk a reduction in the client's agency and capacity to understand their past, present and future in their own terms. Imagine, for instance, that we have a client who continually has relationships with men who are abusive to them. They describe how they always seem to go for 'the bastard', fall in love and then find themselves in a turbulent abusive situation. During the course of therapy we hear about their abusive childhood and it is all too easy to *explain* their current situation being *caused* by this past experience: many forms of therapy embrace this sort of approach, but not the existential approach. Their past will have undoubtedly had an influence on their present situation, we would never deny that, but it does not *determine* who they must be now. Other people have suffered similar abuse in their childhood but are not in abusive relationships as adults, and this particular client also has the capacity to change their present should they have the will (and, of course, support) to do so. It is not likely to be easy but it is possible given their freedom (more on this in Chapter 7). Instead of reducing their past experience to causes we look at them as *reasons* within our descriptive understanding of their total experience and present situation. This allows for different life courses, different choices and different outcomes for our clients that are not *determined* by past events. By focussing on description of the past, present and future we work with their understanding and can then focus on 'how' (the noetic correlate) it affects them.

We should also encourage our clients to describe the 'what' and 'how' of their experience themselves, to engage phenomenologically with their own experience. Many clients will move quickly to explanations without ever properly describing what is going on for them and how it affects them. In the process of explaining their current predicament they might find themselves in a place which feels comfortable, due to its ready familiarity, but given that they are presenting for therapy this is probably not a place that is actually enabling them to live their life to the full. There is often security in explanations; they offer certainty, reduce anxiety, but they may not allow space for the client to change and embrace a new way of living. By encouraging the client to look at their experience phenomenologically we shift the focus from *explanation* to *description* and shine a light on the 'what' and 'how' of their past, present and future. In the process of describing their cyclical abusive relationships the client may come to see their apparent lack of control over their life and feel the frustration that this engenders to the extent that they generate the capacity to effect change. This capacity for change occurs as a client comes to fully understand their world as it is now (inflected as it always is by the past and future possibilities) in all its detail and how this impacts on their capacity to live well now and in the future. As existential therapists we work with our clients through a focus on the 'what' and 'how' of experience to better enable them, through insight, to identify where they might find strength and where they might effect change such that they can live a more fulfilling and satisfying life, in whatever terms they wish.

Activity Work with a partner with each of you taking it in turns to speak about some aspect of your experience for 10 minutes, whilst the other is silent. When listening, see if you can attend to both the 'what' and 'how' of the experience being described. How did you find this process and was it useful to distinguish between the two? After this, you can then move on to the next exercise, with the listener asking, when appropriate, for examples (designed to access the 'what' of experience) and also, when appropriate, 'what was that like?' or a similar question (designed to access the 'how' of experience). Did this help clarify the distinction?

Three structures in phenomenological analysis

Husserl (1900–01/1970) elaborated three forms that recur repeatedly (Sokolowski, 2000) when engaged in a phenomenological analysis, and by understanding these structures our work with clients will be enriched considerably. Sokolowski (2000: 22) describes the three forms as '(a) the structure of *parts and wholes*, (b) the structure of an *identity in a manifold*, and (3) the structure of *presence and absence*'. These three structures are described in detail below and their implications for working as an existential therapist discussed.

There are two different kinds of parts in a whole: pieces and moments. *Pieces* are parts that are independent and can be understood separate from their whole. A person who is a member of a therapy group is, for instance, an *independent* entity though still part of the whole that is the group. Their identity as a person exists independently of the group, even if it might be understood at times within that particular group context. *Moments* are parts that cannot be understood separate from their whole and so are *non-independent* parts. An emotion such as fear or sadness, for instance, is a moment as emotions cannot exist except through the whole of the person who is experiencing that emotion. Moments are blended together into wholes, with some moments being *founding parts* (that is, founded upon other parts). An emotion is founded upon the body, the body provides the substrate for an emotion. One final distinction concerning parts and wholes is between *concretia* and *abstracta*. A whole is a *concretum* as it is something that can be experienced as a concrete individual thing, like a therapy group. A piece can become a *concretum* and be experienced as a concrete individual thing, like the person in a therapy group. A moment, on the other hand, cannot become a *concretum* but is instead an *abstracta*, in that it exists only as blended with other parts. We may talk about an emotion as if it is a concrete thing, but in reality it is a *moment* that can only be truly understood in relation to other parts making up the whole.

So how do these distinctions between parts and wholes make a difference to therapy? Well, in many forms of therapy there are often confusions between pieces and moments. Because we are familiar with talking about emotions as if they were distinct phenomena, and indeed many researchers reduce them to independent variables, we may treat them as if they are discrete concrete entities, as pieces rather than moments. With this they lose their true meaning as they become concretised, with the loss of the complexity of the relationships between moments and the ways in which they are blended together with other parts to form the whole (a person, for instance). In existential therapy, where we work phenomenologically, we must be mindful of this important distinction so that we do not lose sight of the subtleties of meanings when people speak of parts of their lives within the context of the whole of their experience. That is, we seek to work with our clients to understand all aspects of their experience in context. A client's description of an emotion should not be treated as separate from the particular context in which it occurs. So, for instance, if a client describes feeling sad, we should not rush to treat this symptom and lose sight of the meaning of sadness in the context of the totality of the client's experience. Their sadness is not just a symptom but rather something which is revealing about their life and the challenges they are currently facing.

'Manifold' means to have many different forms, features or elements, and the structure of an *identity in a manifold* refers to the multi-faceted nature of our perception of the identity of some aspect of the world. Let me make this clear with an example. Imagine a new client, John, comes to see you for the first time. In the first session you are likely to want some details about John, what he is coming to therapy for, his relevant history and so on. During this encounter you will come to understand more about John, more about his identity through the various manifolds of his world.

He may emerge in this first session as John the capable husband and father, John the successful businessman and John the devoted son. These manifolds reveal his identity, as we perceive it phenomenologically. Later on, however, he may also talk about how he is actually not coping with being the capable husband and father and struggling to keep up with the demands of work, and this new manifold reveals yet another aspect to our perception of his identity. Phenomenology is, in many ways, a process of describing the manifold concerning the object we are interested in: the object for therapists is invariably our client and their experience. Our perception of the identity of any object, be that another person in therapy or something rather more simple like a chair, involves a rich array of manifolds. They will be revealed differently, at different times, and in different settings with different people, but in spite of these differences there will be something in our perception that enables us to continue to identify the object we are perceiving. Our initial perception of John may have been as a capable husband, businessman and son and his identity revealed to us in our intentional relation to him as such. Later, another manifold is revealed with his difficulty coping, but this further elaboration does not change the fact that we are continuing to perceive John. Rather, further elaboration adds another dimension to the way in which we perceive John as our client.

The final structure in a phenomenological analysis concerns *presence* and *absence,* sometimes referred to as 'filled and empty intentions' (Sokolowski, 2000), a reference back to intentionality described above. A filled intention concerns an intention that is bodily present before the one who intends, whilst an empty intention has as it's target something absent (remember that intention in this context refers to the directed nature of consciousness, the idea that consciousness is always of something). If you are not a therapist, then think about being a therapist and what this would be like to experience. Indeed, even if you are a therapist already, think back to when you were not but first thought about becoming a therapist. This is an *empty intention*. The idea is intentionally present to consciousness as you think about it, imagine what it would be like and how it might feel to engage in this kind of activity, but it is what we call an empty intention. However, move forward in time a number of years to meeting your first client as a therapist (or, if you are already a therapist, meeting your next client), and at the moment they enter the consulting room and you experience the actuality of being a therapist in that moment you now have a filled intention. The perceptual reality of the experience is now present for you. Your experience of being a therapist trying to understand the world of your client – in this moment – is referred to in phenomenological terms as your *intuition*. Here intuition is not used to mean some mystical experience but rather simply the moment of having the thing present to you, your consciousness (where you intuit it), rather than absent, of having a filled intention rather than an empty intention. When the client leaves the session and you reflect on the experience, reflect on your understanding of them, you once again have an empty intention, though a different one from your prior (anticipatory) intention before meeting them. This new empty intention is one that is given to memory following a filled intention and is, therefore, distinguishable from those that occur prior to a filled intention. The experience of having an empty versus a filled intention is likely to be different. Imagining a session with a client is very different from actually experiencing a session with a client and still different again from remembering an experience with a client. We might, for instance, imagine what it would be like if we had a client who was very angry or very sad and work through our strategies for dealing with this. The actual experience of being with a client who is very angry or sad may bear some relation to our prior empty intending (in its absence) but will inevitably be different from our imagining of it or our memory of it. Our intention, however, is of the same thing, our client. Our experience of them, in its phenomenological totality, will be a mixture of presences and absences, a mixture of our prior imagining, our actual perception when meeting them, and also our memory of them from previous meetings.

People tend to concentrate on what is present and may, as a consequence, neglect absence, but this is to lose sight of how much of our experience concerns what is absent. When we cannot find something, such as our house keys, they are absent in our intending but matter all the more for this absence. If we are away from home and feel homesick, then our empty intending of our home reveals much about its meaning for us. The same is true when we work therapeutically with clients, for our understanding can only be complete when we pay attention to both their presence as we intend them in the therapy room and also their absence as we intend them before and after a session. The process of clinical supervision relies on this very distinction and is valuable for helping us to work with both the present and absent, in relation with another person, to come to a fuller understanding of our client. This fuller understanding is enriched by our empty intending with our supervisor and the next time we meet them, and they are actually present to us, this empty intending demonstrates its worth, time and again. But it is not just with supervision that the distinction between filled and empty intentions is important. With our clients we need to attend as much to what is absent as that which is present and we can work with them to explore the manifold of their experience using all of the structures above. By working in such detail the full richness of experience is revealed and in this all parts of the whole become clearer such that we and our clients can come to gain much greater insight into their world and any problems they perceive in it.

The phenomenological attitude

Epoché and the natural attitude

In order to engage in phenomenological description we need to set aside our taken-for-granted assumptions about the world, to move away from the *natural attitude* in which we assume a real and knowable world. This is not a denial of a real world existing but rather that in phenomenology our focus must be on the phenomenon itself and how it appears to conscious-ness rather than concerning ourselves with the reality of the thing itself. The first move in this process of setting aside our natural attitude is the *epoché*, sometimes referred to as *bracketing*. Here, we set aside the issue of the reality of the phenomenon we are attending to, along with any other preconceptions, to enable us to better describe the way it appears. The other key element of the epoché when adopting the *phenomenological atti-tude* is that we must also bracket off any theories about the object. We attempt to approach the thing with a naïve sense of wonder, without the prejudices of our culture and history. This would involve us setting aside medical or psychological understandings of a client's life so if they talk of feeling sad we do not label this as depression, with all that that entails, but instead stay with their experience of sadness as it appears. The epoché is, however, controversial and a number of existential philosophers (such as Heidegger and Merleau-Ponty) produced important critiques of this move (more on this in the following chapter). They have questioned how achiev-able it is to stand outside our own way of seeing the world (what is termed the 'transcendental' move in Husserl's phenomenology) and see both poles of the noema–noesis correlation as if we were not a part of it. The critics do not, however, abandon the epoché altogether but rather reformulate it in such a way that it takes proper account of our situated status in time, history, and in our bodies, and how this must be recognised whenever we attempt to understand the way the world appears to us.

The phenomenological reductions

The epoché is the first step in adopting a phenomenological attitude, which is then supplemented (whilst still maintaining the *epoché*) by a series of reductions or rules for how we might better see 'the things in their appear-ing'. The reductions are not clear-cut, as Husserl himself refers to a number of reductions throughout his work, but there is some general con-sensus about the methods we should employ in this process. I draw on Ihde's (1986: 29–54) interpretation of Husserl primarily here, in which three steps are outlined:

- Attend to the phenomenon as it appears.
- Describe, don't explain.
- Horizontalise all phenomena.

The first step in this process may appear obvious but still requires some elaboration here. The focus in this first step is to that which is given to expe-rience. There is, of course, an almost infinite range of possibilities here but the key is that we attend only to that which appears in experience. In therapy we attend to what our clients present to us, focusing on the 'what' and 'how' of their experience, rather than speculation about whether their experience is true or not. So, for instance, if a client tells us about their beliefs, whatever these might be, we take these as a sincere expression of their world view. A client may believe they have been possessed by evil spirits or abducted by aliens: regardless, this is their experience as given and must be treated seriously as such within the phenomenological attitude. This was something that R. D. Laing famously demonstrated when working with people who would be described as suffering from psychosis (where they are out of touch with reality). What Laing (1960, 1961, 1967) showed was how important it was to take expressed experience seriously and not to import theoretical (medical or psychological) frameworks to interpret (and then dismiss) expressions that might seem out of odds with more common understandings of the world. Adams (2001) likens this process in psychotherapy to the *Basic Rule* in Freudian psychoanalysis, where the analyst listens to the analysand (client) with 'even suspended attention' in order to avoid reflection (and any judgements), and also to listen to him- or herself listening. The aim is to gain a 'sense' of the object of attention using our intuition (how it appears to us, as given) rather than by using our judgement or other interpretive framework.

The second step concerning the phenomenological focus on *description* rather than explanation was outlined above in the discussion of the noema-noesis correlation. Description is the primary tool for the phenomenological method and is central in the reduction as the means by which we can see the detail of the object of consciousness with as little prejudice as possible. Once again, Adams (2001) is insightful here about the implications of this rule for psychotherapy, noting that explanations are proportional to the anxiety the therapist is feeling and thus unhelpful, as they invariably increase the client's anxiety and distance the therapist and client from what is going on in the here-and-now of the client's experience. The main danger with description (and indeed the use of phenomenology in general) in psychotherapy is complacency, with the therapist assuming they know what is going on with the client well before they should (this is discussed further below in the section on common misconceptions). The key is to stay, at least initially, with interventions (questions and so on) that focus on the 'what' and 'how' of experience, questions that encourage clients to elaborate the concrete detail of their experience. Ask 'what is it like?' or request an example rather than 'why did you do that?' or responding with 'I understand' too quickly. Obviously, any description will include semantic content, the 'what' of their experience, but we also must not lose sight of the 'how'. One element of the 'how' is the emotional quality of experience, something Adams (2001: 71) argues is vital for full description: 'The dimension of human experience that has the most direct connection with our intentional nature is the emotional dimension. Emotions are what connect us and locate us with our existence'. In the focus on description we need to note the presence and absence of emotions, the quality of the client's emotional life and the impact of their experience on us as therapists. Attending reflexively to one's own emotional state – as much as we attend to our client's emotional world – is a crucial element in existential practice.

Horizontalisation (or the rule of equalisation) is the process by which we seek to keep all phenomenon at the same level in our awareness of them. That is, we do not put things in hierarchies of meaning or importance but instead attempt to treat all objects of consciousness in the same manner. Our own beliefs and values about the world are likely to come to the fore when engaged with clients, and this is where the application of this rule is most important. Even everyday assumptions like the belief that someone should be upset when a parent dies need to be set aside within the phenomenological attitude. A client may talk with great emotional colour about the difficulties in their relationship and say very little about the recent death of a parent, for instance, but we must not assume that there is a problem here for the client in expressing their feelings about loss. They may not have been close to the parent or are more affected emotionally by their relationship difficulties. Or they may, of course, be struggling to come to terms with the death of a parent. We cannot assume we know here until we have stayed with the client's experience sufficiently for their world to reveal itself to us. We keep different elements of a client's experience as expressed on an even level until we have sufficient evidence from the process of epoché and the reductions to know what this means for them.

It is important to note that these steps are the start of the phenomenological attitude in which we attempt to understand the way things appear without prejudice and not the end (the goal, at least according to Husserl, is discussed further in the next section below). It is perfectly legitimate to move from description and horizontalisation to producing hierachies of meanings – and even theories – about the phenomenon, once we have exhausted the reductive process and truly grasped the invariant structure (the essence, see below) of the object we are attempting to understand. Any move beyond description needs to be done with considerable care, however, and should never involve the importation of external concepts (or theories), such as psychoanalytic or cognitive behavioural theory, for instance. All ideas about the object of inquiry must be driven by the way it appears in the phenomenological attitude and any move beyond this should be one of pattern recognition rather than explanatory theory. That is, we might come to produce descriptions of our client's experience in which patterns emerge and key elements become clear, but there is no place for this to be reduced to prior causes (in their childhood or other prior experience) or for us to apply speculative theory to these patterns.

Eidetic intuition (and imaginative variation)

The goal of phenomenology, according to Husserl (1913/1931), is to identify the *essence*, or invariant structure, of the phenomenon we are interested in. That is, we are seeking to find the *eidos* – or the form – of the object of consciousness, as given: this process is, therefore, termed *eidetic intuition*. Perhaps the easiest way to understand this is if we think of trying to understand the structure of a physical object like a table. When we adopt the phenomenological attitude and perceive a table, or rather a series of tables, we seek to identify those qualities that are inherent to all tables – the essence – putting to one side those qualities that vary or are unique to particular tables. We may look at a series of tables and identify an invariant structure in which there are legs and a surface upon which we can place things, putting aside details such as the number of legs, for instance (normally they have four legs but it is quite possible to find a table with three legs), as this quality is not inherent to our understanding of an object as a table. The process of eidetic intuition is the process by which, in this example, we attempt to identify the 'tableness' of the table, the invariant structure that underpins our conceptual understanding of just what it is that makes a table a table.

In therapy we are looking out for common elements in the content and process that may reveal something about the substance of the client's experience, and particularly their underlying beliefs or assumptions, that provide insight into the way in which a particular client may be construing their experience in problematic ways. Adams (2001) suggests two rules of thumb to help the beginning therapist get to grips with this process. The first is to pay attention to an issue that has been mentioned three times or more, and the second is to notice something which lacks emotional tone. Beyond this we may seek to ask questions about whether something has happened before or whether a particular experience reminds a client of some other experience. Through these processes there exists the possibility of patterns emerging in which the *essence* of their experience is revealed. Of course, with experience the therapist is likely to attend in a more subtle way to perceiving patterns, though even here these admittedly simple rules of thumb may be of value. One of the key methods for achieving an eidetic intuition is the process of *free* or *imaginative variation*. Here we seek out sufficient examples of the phenomenon in order to identify that which varies and that which does not (the *essence*), the limit of the experience. This might occur in therapy through a client providing repeated examples of experiences which, to them, result in a damaging personal belief (that they are worthless, for instance). It might also be used by the therapist (either in the session or outside, perhaps in supervision) where they think about a particular client's experience in relation to their experience of other clients discussing similar issues. The variational method is about identifying sufficient empirical examples to provide us with clues about the pattern (or essential structure) of a client's experience. Identifying the essence may be crucial in enabling both client and therapist in recognising key aspects of a client's experience (their beliefs or assumptions, for instance) that underpin behaviour or world views that lead to problems in living.

Adams (2001: 79) identifies three dangers, however, in the application of eidetic intuition that all therapists should reflect upon:

- The common elements must of course belong together by virtue of themselves, and not by virtue of an unexamined assumption of ours about how jigsaws should fit together.
- It is extremely difficult to judge at what point enough evidence has been gathered to justify breaking the rule of horizontalisation and to select a particular item to focus on. This is something that has to be learnt usually through trial and error. Fortunately our clients are usually very patient with our incompetence and clear with their feedback, if we are ready to hear it. We will only know how useful something is by the effect it has, when it is tested.
- Not acknowledging that some elements are more in evidence than others is doing a disservice to yourself and your clients. A reluctance to rely on the authority of your own experience can lead to an idealisation of ignorance. This is the opposite of unknowing, when we are determined not to know. Hiding behind ignorance can be as damaging as hiding behind theory.

Case study   Struggling to comprehend

Amjit came to see me whilst I was working at a counselling centre for younger people because she was struggling with what she saw were serious difficulties in her life around her relationship with her mother and choices about her future. Amjit was 18 years old and lived with her mother in south-east London. When I first met Amjit I found her very charming and remarkably aware of what she was doing in life. The early sessions were promising, with her engaging with therapy and me finding myself drawn into her world. Her world was notably different from mine. She is a young Asian heterosexual woman, living in relative poverty, and I am a white gay man, living in relative comfort, meeting and attempting to forge some common ground. After the first few sessions, however, I found myself struggling to understand what was going on and, in particular, what it was that Amjit wanted to change. I became fixated on change and in the process lost sight of my commitment to understanding her lifeworld and also of our difference, in sex, age, sexuality, experience, knowledge of therapy and so on. This led to frustration on both sides: I became frustrated by an apparent lack of engagement and she became frustrated at my attempts to express my inability to understand what therapy meant to her. This never led to confrontation but rather an awkward relationship, one in which we both took care to maintain a distance. She did not seem to embrace any obvious notion of change and instead filled the sessions with talk about her current life situation and what might unfold in the future. After a number of months I realised, with the help of supervision and also some serious personal reflection, that I was not engaged with Amjit phenomenologically at all. After the first few sessions I had fooled myself into believing that I understood what she needed and then quickly rested on this assumption and sat back, failing to listen to her and failing to offer her a real encounter. Our cultural distance added to this failing on my part, with me too quickly dismissing our difference as I rushed to formulate my understanding. Upon realising my failings I strengthened my efforts to engage with Amjit phenomenologically, rigorously working to understand her experience, whilst setting aside my preconceptions and premature formulation to the best of my ability. This led to a shift, perhaps imperceptible to Amjit but obvious to me, as I felt that I came to know what our differences meant in terms of our expectations about therapy. Amjit was not here to change but instead to explore her future possibilities, to have someone present whilst she struggled with the limits of what was available to her without prejudice or assumption. Whether this would lead to particular choices or changes in her life was not the current concern for Amjit, and when I realised this and moved away from my preconceptions about the purpose of therapy and instead embraced her understanding I felt we moved closer and finally felt I was offering something of value.

Common misconceptions

Phenomenology as empathy

One of the most common mistakes when employing the phenomenological method has been alluded to in Chapter 1 where I discussed the misunderstanding of believing existential counselling and psychotherapy to be just like person-centred counselling. The confusion arises due to the mistake of thinking that the phenomenological method is simply empathic understanding. As I hope you will have realised by reading this chapter, there is much more to the phenomenological method than empathy. Rogers (1980: 115–116) describes empathic understanding as 'the therapist senses accurately the feelings and personal meanings that the client is experiencing and communicates this acceptant understanding to the client.' The phenomenological method does require that the therapist perceive feelings and meaning, as moments that are part of the manifold of human experience. But it is also much more than this, as we must work with our clients on all aspects of their experience, unpacking every element of their understanding of their lifeworld, without the necessity to communicate acceptance back to them. Of course, there will be many times where the therapist does communicate their acceptant understanding back to the client: it would be poor practice not to demonstrate acceptance when therapeutically appropriate (such as early in the therapeutic relationship when establishing rapport with a client), but there will also be times when this does not occur but instead the client is expected to stand alone in order to take charge of their own understanding of the world. There will also be many times when an existential therapist will do more than simply communicate acceptant understanding: there will be times when the therapist engages the client in debate (about some belief, for instance), where this is thought to be therapeutic in challenging aspects of their understanding that are leading to problems in how they live their life.

Failing to meet the needs of the client

The opposite tendency to that of seeing phenomenology as empathy is to fail to meet the needs of the client, to present a cold presence hidden behind the mask of 'the professional', where the client feels unheard and unmet in the therapeutic relationship. Whilst there is no necessity for empathy or warmth in the phenomenological method, ideas from other philosophers (such as Martin Buber, discussed in detail in Chapter 8) and knowledge from therapists who have translated phenomenological philosophy into a therapeutic method, suggests that we need to have the capacity to meet our clients with warmth and understanding. There are exceptions to this with, for instance, the Daseinsanalysts, modelling themselves on classical psychoanalysis, adopting the distant style of the psychoanalyst, offering a presence, and interventions when appropriate, but little in the way of empathy or warmth (though this is not the case with all Daseinsanalysts, of course, and Boss himself referred to the need for warmth in the therapeutic relationship). However, within the British school the norm is to work reflectively, drawing on the evidence base concerning the value of the therapeutic relationship alongside philosophical understanding, to ensure that a productive relationship can be established. This is likely, with most clients, to involve us expressing acceptant understanding, empathy and warmth early on in the relationship (and also later when felt appropriate). This should be genuine warmth, not contrived or acted, but the warmth that emerges naturally between two human beings who meet within the context of a caring relationship. But within this caring relationship there must always be room for challenge and also, most importantly, room for the client to struggle alone, to draw on their own strength to meet whatever difficulties in living they are facing. These are subtle distinctions, but important ones that enable us to offer our clients something more than simply acceptant understanding, such that the client's desires for change, strength and engagement with life become realisable.

Mistakes in the use of bracketing: 'I understand you now'

There are dangers in the naïve use of phenomenology, notably in thinking that all of the therapist is set to one side through the epoché and reduction, and that they truly know (as if it were their own experience) what the world is like for their client. Whilst Husserl, in his later writing in particular, believed that it was possible to transcend our own situation in the world and see things beyond our own perspective, this position has been heavily criticised (by Heidegger, amongst others, discussed in detail in the next chapter). This does not mean that we should not attempt to move beyond our own natural attitude and try to engage with the phenomenological attitude instead, but rather that this is always an imperfect process, especially when trying to understand the most complex of things that we can ever perceive – another human being. We can never truly experience the world of another person but through the systematic application of ideas from phenomenology we can get as close as possible to understanding the other. We must, however, always recognise that we meet the other in a particular context (the here-and-now of a particular therapeutic relationship at a particular moment in time between one client and one therapist) and this context will have an impact on our encounter. If we are not rigorous in our application of the phenomenological method it is all too easy for us to project our own subjectivity onto our clients, to fail to understand their world view but instead see what we want to see. This slip into the projection of the therapist's subjectivity onto the client is one of the reasons why it is important for all existential therapists to have engaged in a sustained period of personal reflection, often through their own personal therapy, and furthermore suggests that the key criterion for suitability to become an existential therapist is openness to views beyond one's own. People thinking about working as an existential therapist need personal insight, the capacity to reflect on their own beliefs and values, alongside a genuine willingness to understand the other in a non-judgemental manner. The phenomenological method allows us to come to understand another person, but that is dependent on how seriously we approach the task of being a therapist and how willing and able we are to carry this out effectively.

Case study   Uncovering that which is not immediately apparent

I saw Tom privately for a relatively short period of time (six months), a period in which he moved from one of isolation into one of relation. Tom had HIV and appeared, at first at least, to have faced his diagnosis with considerable courage and positivity. Our work, however, quickly revealed how his diagnosis had resulted in him avoiding relationships of any significance. It would have been easy to miss this pattern as it was not something Tom himself recognised, and indeed his positive outlook on his HIV status was admirable. It was through the phenomenological method that I was able to work with Tom to reveal aspects of his experiencing process that had hitherto been hidden to him, in spite of the way that they impacted negatively on his life. He presented because of his 'workaholism' (his term) and how he wanted to gain a better 'work–life balance'. Tom worked in the City and seemingly spent a considerable amount of his time working, climbing the corporate ladder and forging a very successful career. He had a wide network of friends who he would see at weekends, mostly for a night of hardcore drinking, drugging and clubbing. At first his lifestyle sounded seductive: he had a huge disposable income, a penthouse flat in London, a wide social circle and casual sex as and whenever he wanted it. He worked very hard but my initial impression of Tom was that his life was pretty much in order and that this was likely to be some very brief work (we agreed to see each other for six sessions initially) simply to address his need for 'a little more down time from work'. The first couple of sessions mostly focussed on his work life and associated pressures, with little mention of the rest of his life above and beyond that which he told me in the first session. It looked like our work would indeed be concerned simply with dealing with his presenting concern of addressing the work–life balance. I noticed an absence regarding the lack of an intimate relationship but set this aside in order to avoid imposing my assumptions about the quality of having intimate

(Continued)

(Continued)

relationships, but held on to this absence in the light of my awareness that attending to presence and absence is a key aspect of a phenomenological perspective. Over the course of the next few sessions Tom mentioned more than once feeling lonely but not having enough time for a relationship, and with this I broke the rule of horizontalisation and asked whether he wanted a relationship and what this would mean for him. At first, he reiterated his lack of time and need for such a relationship, but then talked (gradually, over a number of sessions) about the impact of his HIV diagnosis on him and his fears about people not wanting to form a relationship with him as a consequence of this. We discussed his experience of telling people about having HIV and some of the difficult experiences he had encountered. We also talked about how he had erected a protective wall around himself to ward off the danger of experiencing such difficulties in the future, and how this worked well but also shut off an element of the world to him. Towards the end of our brief work he acknowledged a need to start to take some more risks, letting down his protective wall, in order to realise the possibility of an intimate relationship. He knew this would not be easy but felt that it was something he needed to do. I wished him well with this new challenge and affirmed his courage in taking such a risk. Our work together reminded me of the value of the phenomenological method but also of the need to think through presence and absence and for the therapist to take risks (whilst working phenomenologically, of course), even in brief work, if they are to provide the best service to their clients. A naïve phenomenological stance, that did not take account of the detail of the phenomenological method outlined in this chapter, might have led to me failing to identify the absence and ask about this aspect of his life. By understanding the complexity of the phenomenological method and using this in practice we are better able to work with our clients to look at their lives such that what is not immediately apparent to them may be revealed.

Further reading

Ashworth, P. & Cheung Chung, M. (Eds) (2006). *Phenomenology and psychological science*. New York: Springer.
  A very interesting edited collection on phenomenology and psychology (including psychotherapy), which includes a number of chapters providing excellent further reading on phenomenology and psychotherapy.

Moran, D. (2000). *Introduction to phenomenology*. London: Routledge.
  A dense but extremely scholarly book providing comprehensive detail about Husserl and a range of other thinkers in the phenomenological movement.

Sokolowski, R. (2000). *Introduction to phenomenology*. Cambridge: Cambridge University Press.
  An extremely clear and succinct introduction to the detail of Husserl's phenomenology. It does not provide comprehensive references to Husserl's own texts throughout so is probably best augmented by another text which does this, but it does provide a beautiful introduction to this often complex body of thought.

THREE   The Development of Existential Therapy

CHAPTER AIMS

This chapter aims to:

- provide an introduction to the fundamentals of existential philosophy;
- discuss the existential revision of phenomenology and its implications for practice.

The fundamentals of existential philosophy

Existentialism as a school of philosophy is difficult to pin down, with a number of philosophers beyond the core group of existentialists working with existential ideas, and indeed some of those now widely considered to be existentialists refusing the label in their own lifetime. Warnock (1970), however, provides a helpful way of marking off what should be considered existential philosophy in terms of two key principles: a concern with human freedom and a fundamentally practical approach to philosophy. To quote Warnock herself (1970: 1–2):

> They are all of them interested in the world considered as the environment of man [sic], who is treated as a unique object of attention, because of his power to choose his own course of action. ... the problem of freedom is in a sense a practical problem. They aim, above all, to show people *that they are free*, to open their eyes to something which has always been true, but which for one reason or another may not always have been recognised, namely that men [sic] are free to choose, not only what to do on a specific occasion, but what to value and how to live.

There would be little debate about these two criteria being central to all existential philosophy and, indeed, also existential therapy. With this in mind there are two traditions that have led to the foundation of existentialism proper: the ethical philosophy of Søren Kierkegaard (1813–1855) and Friedrich Nietzsche (1844–1900), and the phenomenological method of Husserl (discussed in detail in the previous chapter). The root of existential philosophy in the work of Kierkegaard and Nietzsche is discussed below, but before this it is worth spending a little more time explaining the relationship between existentialism and phenomenology. In my view, there cannot be an existential therapy without phenomenology. As discussed in the previous two chapters, phenomenology provides the method for existential therapy that then enables the therapist to draw on ideas from existential philosophy. Similarly, for philosophers such as Warnock there can be no existential philosophy without the phenomenological method: she sees the phenomenological method as the third criterion necessary for philosophical work to be considered existential. However, this results in a relatively limited number of philosophers falling within the existential tradition, as defined by Warnock: Heidegger, Merleau-Ponty and Sartre being the notable examples. These three philosophers are without doubt the thinkers who provide the heart of existentialism, and are also the most associated with the tradition. A number of other contemporary writers would argue that employing all three criteria (especially the need for philosophers to use the phenomenological method themselves to be classed as existentialists) is too limiting, with too much work that is in the true spirit of existentialism excluded for not embracing the phenomenological method (Buber, Jaspers, Tillich, Marcel, Frankl and Camus being the obvious examples). I think this is true also, and whilst the three criteria of Warnock (1970) provide a useful indicator of the limits of existentialism, the necessity for philosophers to use the phenomenological method to be classed as existentialists is too restrictive. The three criteria are, however, in my view necessary conditions (when translated into therapeutic practise) to be classed as an existential therapist. In the following sections I first outline the roots of existential philosophy in the work of Kierkegaard and Nietzsche and then move on to consider the work of Heidegger, whose work forms the heart of existentialism and also existential therapy. The work of the philosophers most popularly associated with existentialism – Sartre, de Beauvoir and Merleau-Ponty – is considered, alongside other work, in Part II where I discuss specific elements of their thought and the implications for therapy.

Roots of existential philosophy

Søren Kierkegaard is generally considered the father of existentialism (Warnock, 1970; Dreyfus, 2009) with other earlier philosophers such as, for instance, the ancient Greek philosopher Heraclitus (535–475 BC) and the famous French mathematician and philosopher Blaise Pascal (1623–1662) more properly thought of as 'proto-existentialists' (Dreyfus, 2009). Kierkegaard's work and life are inextricably linked with his philosophy reflecting his own journey through life and, in his own terms, serving as a 'singular universal' – a simple project of personal reflection – which, through 'divine Governance', has become of universal significance for all people engaged in personal reflection on the meaning of life. Much of Kierkegaard's rhetoric speaks to the work of Georg Hegel (1770–1831), and also in many ways that of Immanuel Kant (1724–1804), and is concerned primarily with religion and faith. Both Kant and Hegel embraced a rationalist approach to understanding fundamental questions of ethics and knowledge. Kierkegaard's work offers a profound challenge to the work of both philosophers, though his principal target was Hegel, with Kierkegaard rejecting Hegel's rationalism as the way to become closer to God, and therefore truth, and the notion of scientific knowledge as the means to man's redemption. In the following discussion I present some of the key concerns of Kierkegaard with less emphasis on the religious element than one might – given its centrality in his thought – in order to highlight the ideas for all therapists (and clients), whether they are religious or not.

Kierkegaard (1843a/1992, 1843b/1985) identifies three stages in existential development, reflecting three stages he seemingly moved through in his own life: the aesthetic, the ethical and the religious. The aesthetic stage is one characterised by sensuous immersion in the world, irony and flight from boredom and a focus on possibilities rather than actuality. This stage is best characterised in Kierkegaard's writing (1843a/1992) by the figure of *Johannnes*, a seducer, in *Either/Or*. For Johannes it is not the act of seduction that appeals so much as the process by which he engineers such possibilities. Such activities are by their nature self-serving, devoid of any notion of community and responsibility and are thus criticised from the point of view of ethics. This stage is, in Kierkegaard's terms, a fantastical way of protecting oneself from *angst*, the despair or anxiety that must be faced through recognition of the freedom and responsibility inherent to existence.

The ethical stage is necessary before one might reach the religious stage (discussed below) and is seen by Kierkegaard as a further limited stage of existence in which one unreflectively thinks and acts in accordance with the prevailing social norms. Here, unlike the aesthetic stage, one demonstrates a commitment to the social world, moving beyond the self-serving interests of the individual aesthete. The motivation to act ethically stems from angst, rather than by thinking through the meaning of actions for oneself and so the rules one abides by are arbitrary, concealed through apparently rational communication and socio-political dialogue. For Kierkegaard, the organised Church in Denmark represented this stage through dogmatic thinking and a false belief in the ability to come closer to God through such ways of acting.

The religious stage incorporates aspects of both prior stages, albeit transformed, with the possibilities of aesthetic imagination and the ethical sense of social commitment realised through a personal subjective passion. It is the freedom of subjectivity that results in angst, as each individual must make choices for themselves for eternity, provoking dread as a result of the burden but also exhilaration at the possibility of choice. It was individual faith that comes about as a result of subjective passion, rather than doctrine through the teachings of the Church, which forms the most important task for human being. Faith is the means by which one achieves a sense of authentic selfhood, which can then be judged in eternity by God. Movement through these stages cannot come about through persuasion or coercion as each person must decide how to live their life themselves, but the evangelical[1] spirit at the heart of existentialism is clear with Kierkegaard, as it is with the next key figure in early existentialism to be discussed here, Nietzsche. Putting aside the question of faith and religion in Kierkegaard's philosophy, the key distinction throughout Kierkegaard's work is between *subjectivity* and *objectivity*. Objectivity, in Kierkegaard's terms, is 'the tendency to accept rules governing both behaviour and thought' (Warnock, 1970: 8) and any discipline which attempts to explain, generalise and predict (such as much academic psychology or indeed morality given to us through universal rules) is therefore objective. The rejection of scientism – the view that science alone provides truths about the world – is common to most existentialists with subjectivity prised instead. Subjectivity here refers to the ability to think for ourselves and live our lives in 'inwardness', where we make choices knowingly with passion rather than accept the norms given to us without reflection.

Friedrich Nietzsche offered a similar challenge to objective thought (and in particular, conventional morality) but his philosophy was, in contrast to Kierkegaard, profoundly anti-theistic. His work, like that of many Continental philosophers, has been read in different ways by other philosophers and it is therefore impossible to provide a definitive description of all of his thinking. In the following section I set out the fundamentals and allude to some of the debates around the meaning of his thought but focus predominantly on the way in which his work has influenced existential thinking and, most importantly, the practice of existential therapy.

A rejection of objectivity is common to both Kierkegaard and Nietzsche, with the latter arguing that there are 'no facts, only interpretations'. As such, Nietzsche is regarded as advocating *perspectivism*, with science and moral law alike targets of his attacks for their (mythical) foundational nature. Nietzsche argued instead that all values are the product of human attempts to control and manipulate the world, characteristic of beings which demonstrate the *will to power* and thus have the capacity to deliberately change their situation. The will to power is a controversial aspect of Nietzsche's philosophy, with many different interpretations of its meaning and criticisms of its place in his philosophy, particularly his perspectivism (see Doyle, 2001, for a discussion and defence). Some have interpreted the will to power in psychological terms (effectively as individual will-power), though this is mistaken and will to power should more properly be understood in terms of the force that drives or motivates all sentient beings to effect change in their world. All perceptions of the world are laden with valuations (for example,

---

[1]Meaning, in this case, characterised by ardent or crusading enthusiasm, rather than being in accordance with Christian gospel.

good or bad, true or false, acceptable or unacceptable) and thus any claims to objective neutrality are false, in terms of the capacity to build a systematic body of knowledge that is true for all time. This is not to say that there is no value at all in the objective study of the world through the natural sciences, for instance, but rather recognition that the claims of such objective disciplines need to be tempered by the knowledge that they reflect the practical desire to control the world rather than provide some foundational truth.

In *The Gay Science* (1882/1972) Nietzsche proclaims the *death of God* as a reaction against an all-knowing judgemental authority and salvation through heavenly redemption and towards an atheism, which necessarily requires recognition (and action in the light) of the inherent freedom in one's presently experienced world. He also expounds the notion of *eternal recurrence*, the possibility of being reborn again and again to experience life's events as chosen and lived for all eternity, for two reasons. The first, in line with the proclamation of the death of God, is to stress the need for us to recognise our life as lived now, in this singular world (rather than through any escape from the present world). The second is as a marker of psychological health through people's different reactions to the notion of eternal recurrence. That is, this concept revolves around a thought experiment about the ability to be able to live one's life again and again, feeling satisfied with the choices one has made. For Nietzsche this was a key marker of psychological health as people living in the present world, knowingly choosing their fate in the face of the fear of such freedom, would be able to live with their choices satisfactorily for eternity.

His next work, *Thus Spoke Zarathustra, A Book for All and None* (1883–85/2003), is probably his most well-known and controversial, where he draws out his ideas about a higher mode of being, referred to as the overman or super-human (*übermensch*). The overman is associated with the doctrine of eternal recurrence as the healthiest way of living, loving one's life for all eternity and able to stand over those beings immersed in the everyday conditions of human existence, those living within *the herd* rather than in full awareness of the true human condition. This work also represents Nietzsche's clearest explanation of his perspectivism and the rejection of any absolute standpoint from which one can judge human affairs.

There is a practical and missionary[2] quality to Nietzsche's writing, in common with that of all the existentialists. His aim was to transform the world and enable those that were able to recognise the cultural illusions (namely the immutable nature of science and moral law) in which they lived. There is an elitism, represented best by his notorious notion of the masters (or shepherds) that shall impose their will on the slaves (or herd), in Nietzsche that is distinctly problematic. However, his overarching message of the need to think about one's place in the world, to recognise our

---

[2]Meaning here, the tendency to propagandise or use insistent persuasion rather than religious missionary activity.

ability to choose our path, and act accordingly, is one that is central in the thought of the existentialists which followed him (discussed below). For Nietzsche and Kierkegaard, a sense of personal enlightenment, of insight into the cultural illusions of the world we inhabit, is the answer for how we can live well in the face of the problems of life, to realise ourselves fully should we wish to, and this is true for all other existential philosophers and also forms the fundamental basis of existential therapy.

Case study   Anita and Jane

Anita came to see me for training therapy[3] with few presenting concerns. Our work continued for several years and during that time a number of substantive issues arose, including her relationship with Jane. Anita was a lesbian who had had relatively few partners in her life and now felt that this was not a priority for her. She had a full life with many friends and felt that her newly developing career in psychotherapy was the most important thing for her at that time. She spoke frequently of her close relationship with Jane, who she considered her best friend and confidant. After a few months Anita suddenly announced that she was thinking of asking Jane to be her civil partner. They lived in different cities in the UK and had never had sex together but Jane thought that this made perfect sense. She had previously thought that they might live together and could imagine herself happy without needing sexual intimacy. This was in fact not a snap decision by Anita but was something she had thought long and hard about. She wanted to publicly affirm her relationship with Jane and thought that this was something Jane would also want. She had some doubts about whether this was legitimate or whether she was just 'copping out' of having a 'real partner' who she lives with and has sex with. I was reminded of Kierkegaard's notion of living in inwardness and the need for each person to make choices which were grounded in their own sense of what was right rather than any socially determined expectations. I asked Anita about the source of her doubts and it became clear that this was due to her recognition that this would not be a traditional relationship and so would be at odds with social expectations. We explored whether this mattered and during this she came to recognise that this was right for her. She worried about the risk that she would be taking in asking Jane and how it might damage the relationship, but she felt it was worth it as her motive was based on her love and care for Jane and simply reflected her desire for greater openness and recognition of their already close relationship. There was a Nietzschean awareness of the fullness of Anita's own life and I reflected this back to her, speaking of how she was – at this moment – clearly in touch with her own experiencing process, even if it seemed at odds with social norms (of the herd). I was impressed by the passion being expressed and Anita's courage to take the risk to reveal more of herself to Jane and face the consequences – good or bad – with the necessary fortitude.

---

[3]She was herself training to become a therapist and so had to undergo therapy herself, referred to as 'training therapy'.

The heart of existentialism

The work of Martin Heidegger (1889–1976) in many ways represents the heart of existential thinking, in spite of Heidegger's own refusal to be labelled an existentialist. Heidegger's philosophical project was quite different from Husserl (see Chapter 2). Whilst Husserl sought to identify what we could know about the world – an epistemological project (*epistemology*: the philosophical study of knowledge, or what we can know) – and developed an elaborate methodology to enable us to better grasp the essence of experience, Heidegger was concerned with a more fundamental question of what is *Being* itself – an ontological project (*ontology*: the philosophical study of Being, or of what exists). This may seem a strange question but it is a fundamental one in philosophy for what we can know; that is, all our descriptions and understandings of things in the world depend on things existing in the first place, and philosophers like Heidegger have been concerned with trying to understand the nature of Being itself: 'Why are there beings at all, and why not rather nothing?' (Heidegger, 1947/1993: 110). But why is this seemingly obscure philosophical concern important for existential therapy? Well, the method by which Heidegger attempted to answer this question was to examine the detail of *human being* as a particular example of Being-in-general. This was simply because he believed that human being was unique, as we are the only things that exist which ask questions about the nature of existence itself (about Being-in-general). This resulted in a comprehensive examination of human being and as a result provides tremendous insight into the human condition, which is of value for those of us working therapeutically with others engaged in a personal struggle to live. Note the important distinction here between human being (without a capital 'b') and Being-in-general (with a capital 'B'): human being is just one example of Being and the question of Being-in-general concerns all things that exist rather than just humans.

Heidegger (1927/1962) does not refer to human beings per se in his exploration of being but instead uses the term *Dasein* (and in the later writings of Heidegger appears as *Da-sein*). Dasein is a commonly used German word often translated as 'presence' but Heidegger uses it to refer to 'there-being' (or more commonly in English, 'being-there'), the place of openness where being occurs. This concept is difficult to grasp at first as it does not refer to a place or object in space but is instead an attempt to move away from any notion of persons as fixed, capsule-like entities, with minds separate from bodies and consciousness separate from the world:

> The new 'ground' of human existence should be called 'Da-sein' (Being there) or 'Being-in-the-world'. The 'there' of this Being-there does, however, not mean – as it does colloquially – a position in space near to the viewer. Rather existence as 'Da-sein' means the opening up of a sphere where the sense of what is given can be perceived. Human 'Da-sein' – as a sphere of potentiality of perception and awareness – is never an object that is just present. It is, on the contrary, under no circumstances something that can be objectified. (Heidegger, 1987/2001: 3–4)

This radical move is only the start of Heidegger's project, but in itself represents a significant shift in thinking about the nature of what existence is for human beings or, more properly, Dasein. Existence is open, not fixed, and always already in relation to the world. There is no gap between persons and world, as is found with those philosophies following Descartes (see Chapter 2), in the spirit of Husserl's development of the notion of intentionality, an important influence on Heidegger's work. The relationship between Heidegger's philosophy and Husserl's phenomenology is discussed more fully in the following section. In therapy, therefore, we are not focussed on what is going on inside the client's head per se but rather on their experience of their world as a whole, as expressed in the therapeutic relationship. The aim is not to reduce the whole of a client's life to psychological parts but to work with them to uncover more and more elements of their experience to shed light on the way in which they live now, such that new possibilities are opened up in awareness. This is a subtle but important shift in focus that is in line with the phenomenological tradition of attending to the things in their appearing (rather than reducing the totality of experience to diagnostic labels, individual cognitions or reductive interpretations) and one which marks out existential therapy from most other forms of therapy.

With the clue in the title of Heidegger's (1927/1962) masterpiece *Being and Time*, *temporality* is the essence of human being. We understand ourselves in the present through recollecting the past and projecting ourselves into the future. Temporality is key with past and future inseparable from the present as Dasein projects itself towards future possibilities. Existence is not a static series of moments but always open to realising possibilities within the web of time. We are not fixed or determined like a stone but ever changing and engaged in realising our possibilities. Such possibilities are not limitless, however, for we are *thrown* into the world and find ourselves in a given situation. Environmental, physical, social, cultural and psychological factors limit us and provide the *facticity* of existence for Dasein. Our facticity never determines who or what we can be, however, as this too is part of our possibility. We make the world meaningful through our facticity and our response to it and as a result make the world our own.

Heidegger (1927/1962) distinguishes between *ontological* and *ontic* aspects of human being. Ontological aspects concern those aspects of Being-in-general that are given and inescapable for all human beings – sometimes referred to as *existentials*, and are his main focus, as he works towards his aim of understanding Being-in-general. These include such things as Being-in-the-world (or concern), facticity (or thrownness), mood, being-in-world-with-others, mortality, spatiality, temporality and embodiment. To take the last existential, embodiment, it is an inescapable given of human existence that we inhabit bodies and through this come to know the world. Each of us, however, may respond differently to these existentials as we create our own meaning in the world, and this is the realm of the *ontic*. All human beings have a basic grasp of existentials (the ontological aspects of Being) but most often live everyday primarily concerned with the ontic. As such, ontological aspects of existence are revealed to an existential therapist primarily through the ontic concerns of the client, their everyday experience of life. Heidegger (1987/2001) himself warns against a rush from the ontic to the ontological in therapy: ontic concerns must be treated seriously in themselves and it is important not to rush too quickly to the ontological when a client reveals their experience in therapy.

Concern or *care* (*Sorge*, in German), for Heidegger (1927/1962), is a fundamental element of Dasein and concerns the significance that human being has for Dasein. This is sometimes represented through the hyphenated term 'Being-in-the-world', which expresses the way in which we are always part of the world, inseparable from it through our concern. Beyond this we also experience the world through our pre-reflective *moods* or *attunement* (*Stimmungen*). This concept is broader than our everyday psychological understanding of mood but suggests that all our experience (how the world is revealed to Dasein) is through Dasein's mood. Our mood is not simply a response to events in the world but also provides the lens through which we experience the world and is not therefore reducible to causes of a particular mood. On an ontic level we experience moods as feelings (Cohn, 2002) and they offer clues to how we are experiencing the world, disclosing our world view. They therefore form an essential part of the existential therapeutic practice. Attending to a person's feelings is key in understanding how they approach the world and what it means to them. They provide insight into aspects of a person's experiencing process that is often out of conscious reflection and form an essential counterpoint to reflective philosophical discussion about the way they are living their life.

Heidegger (1927/1962) distinguishes between an *authentic self* (*eigentlichen selbst*) and the *they-self* (*Man-selbst*) to highlight the contrast between a Dasein that has grasped and fully embraced their own being and one which is lost in the inauthentic activities of life and the social world into which they are thrown. There is considerable confusion over the meaning of 'authentic', at least in part due to the translation of the term from German, and the associated meaning of the English term (Cohn, 2002). Authenticity and inauthenticity are existentials that form part of human being, with most people living inauthentically most of the time as they are caught up in the 'they' of everyday life. This does not mean authenticity is genuineness (and inauthenticity falseness) or is a better way of living as Heidegger strives to avoid such associations:

> This inauthentic self-understanding ... by no means signifies an ungenuine self-understanding. On the contrary, this everyday having of self within our factical, existent, passionate merging into things can surely be genuine, whereas all extravagant grubbing about in one's soul can be in the highest degree counterfeit ... Dasein's inauthentic understanding of itself via things is neither ungenuine or illusory as though what is understood by it is not the self but something else. (Heidegger, 1982, cited in Cohn, 2002: 88).

Authentic and inauthentic clearly do not imply a distinction between a real (or genuine) self and false self but simply represent different aspects of human being. *Existential anxiety (angst)* is what leads to inauthenticity, as we protect ourselves from our *being-towards-death* by immersion in the everyday activities of life. Anxiety presents Dasein with a challenge we may face or avoid. I use the word 'challenge' here as such anxiety (the product of our awareness of our own Being) may not simply be negative but enable us to realise possibilities as we creatively face it through our choices and actions in the world. Death is the ultimate culmination of life for all human beings, as we are beings in time, and therefore marks the end of our possibilities. Our awareness of the finite quality of life and the inevitability of death is the source of this existential anxiety (angst), the most fundamental of all existential moods. In existential therapy authenticity is not, therefore, a goal but instead should be seen as another existential that may become ontically apparent, where a client may fail to face a life challenge that confronts them due to the anxiety it provokes and then leads to dissatisfaction. That is, a client may struggle to move from living in their everydayness (inauthentically as part of *das Man*) when their desire is to realise some aspect of their being authentically due to the anxiety this provokes, and here the existential therapist may be able to offer the necessary support to enable them to effect change in their world. The desire must belong to the client, as all of us live contentedly with inauthenticity for much of our lives.

The final element of Heidegger's thought that I will discuss here concerns his understanding of *relatedness* (sometimes called *intersubjectivity*) or *Being-with*. For Dasein the world is a with-world as we are always in the world with others (*Being-with* or *being-in-the-world-with-others*). The ontological starting point for human being is relatedness. This is an *existential* and so forms the ground for human being but may be experienced ontically in very different ways. It was a confusion between the ontic and ontological with this issue and the notion of concern that led Binswanger to develop his theory of loving relatedness, which Heidegger thought – though an interesting idea – fundamentally misunderstood the ontological nature of his ideas about relatedness (see Cohn, 2002, for more on this). Heidegger is not talking about the ontic manifestation of relatedness here but rather the universal and so everyday aspects of our experience of relationships (love, hatred and so on) are not discussed. This does not mean they are not important to Heidegger or existential therapists but rather that they did not form part of his project to elucidate the nature of Being-in-general.

Heidegger (1927/1962) does, however, develop his notion of being-with when he discusses two forms of *solicitude* (*Fürsorge*), an idea related to concern (*Sorge*) that expresses the concern of one Dasein for another. Heidegger discusses *deficient modes of solicitude* such as being against one another, passing by another and not mattering for another, and contrasts these with two positive modes of solicitude: *leaping in* and *leaping ahead*. To *leap in* for another Dasein is where we take control of their situation for them to help them and then return control to them once the issue is addressed. This is akin to the traditional medical model where a doctor takes control of the presenting difficulty and through drugs attempts to cure the illness. *Leaping ahead* is where one Dasein does not take the concern for their being of the other away but helps them to better realise it him- or herself. This is generally considered the focus of existential therapy, where the therapist works to enable clients to understand their situations and gain control of it themselves.

Case study   Being towards death

Jane came to see me as she was suffering from an overwhelming sense of low mood. She was in her sixties, married with one child and two grandchildren, and had recently moved home. It appeared that moving home had triggered something in Jane that took her by surprise. Jane had been very active throughout her life, always filling her time with some activity. She worked successfully for many years as a teacher, spent considerable time travelling, amongst many other activities. She had retired a few years ago and threw herself into gardening and the various clubs she belonged to. It was moving house that precipitated this sudden change in Jane's mood. She was utterly puzzled by these events as she remained able to continue in her clubs and spend time looking after her grandchildren, 'nothing has changed'. She now even had a bigger garden to work on. It became apparent that whilst nothing has ostensibly changed in Jane's life, her recent move signalled a shift in her sense of self, 'a final house move before death'. Jane had never considered her own mortality before, always keeping herself busy. Indeed, it was her husband who was preoccupied with his mortality, expressed through some degree of hypochondriasis and anxiety about himself and others that he cared about. Jane had always been a counter to this position, deflecting any anxieties through activities. Whilst she was still potentially able to be as active as ever, the recent house move had forced her to confront her own mortality through the image of the move being their last. Of course, in reality they might be able to move again should they wish, but her fantasy was that this was the 'beginning of the end'. I needed to be mindful of the danger of leaping in for Jane, offering up practical advice about keeping herself busy and counters to her sudden awareness of death. She needed to confront her anxiety if it was to subside. We stayed with her anxiety and talked practically about ageing and the changes that were inevitable, alongside those possibilities that remained. Her low mood resulted from her own belief that opportunities in her life were closing down. In time, Jane accepted that her shift in mood was a necessary process of coming to terms with her age and acknowledged that her 'keeping busy' defence was inevitably time-limited. Life may need to slow down, though not right now, and she would need to find different ways of keeping herself occupied. Her mood lifted slowly as she began to accept her being-toward-death, recognising that whilst there is a limit to life this is better faced with passion – 'to live what is left to the full' – than avoided through her low mood and removal of herself from her world.

Phenomenology and existentialism: the lifeworld (*Lebenswelt*)

It is worth now returning to phenomenology (outlined in detail in the previous chapter) to look once again at the relationship between phenomenology and existentialism. Husserl's phenomenology, particularly his transcendental move with the epoché and reductions, came under sustained critique from a number of existential philosophers, notably Heidegger (1927/1962). Husserl's (1936/1970) notion of the *lifeworld*, however, was an important concept that he started to develop in his later work that prefigured the work of the existentialists in moving phenomenology from a transcendental phenomenology to an existential phenomenology. The lifeworld was, for Husserl, the pre-given physical, social, cultural (and so on) aspects of the world that underpin someone's natural attitude, effectively the system of meanings expressed through language, that serve to ground consciousness. This move to situate consciousness more properly in the world is in many ways the essence of Heidegger's own phenomenological project (see MacDonald, 2001, for a defence of Husserl against the existentialist critiques). Heidegger's own approach, an existential-phenomenology, was of course informed by Husserl but was much less systematic with no role for the epoché or reductions. It involved a rejection of the notion of a detached observer who could transcend or step outside the experience and describe the invariant structures of experience (the universal essence of the things in their appearing). Alongside this it entailed recognition of the inevitably historical and cultural nature of all human experience, with experience situated (at an ontic level) in a particular personal context. Analysis on this basis should therefore be hermeneutic, interpretive, in the sense of extending what is already known rather than replacing it with some more basic idea or element. Here we do not strip away the individual variations or reduce their meaning to something more basic but further elucidate these unique meanings and expand our understanding. Cohn (2002) does not see the epoché and reductions as incompatible with Heidegger's methodological shift but instead recognises their value in enabling us to stay close to the provisional nature of hermeneutic interpretation that is about revealing more of Dasein's experience and is never final. Cohn (2002) was mistaken in thinking that the reductions, described as rules or steps by Spinelli, were not fundamental to Husserl and his philosophical project, but is right that there are ways of employing aspects of Husserl's phenomenological method within an existential-phenomenological investigation. The epoché and search for invariant properties are arguably the methods that conflict with Heidegger's philosophy, but even here there are ways for the existential therapist to work that resolve (in practice, at least) this conflict. The epoché is an aim, not achievable in totality, that actually helps the therapist to focus on Dasein and what being means for any individual. The connection between this and the goal of identifying essences for Husserl does not fit with Heidegger's philosophy but, as indicated in the previous chapter, invariant structures can be seen as patterns that the experienced therapist may identify. Such patterns identified across clients (as a product of experience on the part of the therapist) may be valuable within the therapeutic process as long as they are provisional and always open to revision as the therapist works to explore the way the world appears for any individual client.

Further reading

Cohn, H. (2002). *Heidegger and the roots of existential therapy.* London: Continuum.
> A beautifully clear, simple and accurate account of Heidegger's thought and the implications of it for existential therapy.

Dreyfus, H. L. & Wrathall, M. A. (2009). *A companion to phenomenology and existentialism.* Chichester: Wiley-Blackwell.
> A comprehensive overview of existentialism and phenomenology with chapters written by some of the leading contemporary philosophers in the field.

Halling, S. & Dearborn Nill, J. (1995). A brief history of existential-phenomenological psychiatry and psychotherapy. *Journal of Phenomenological Psychology, 26*(1), 1–45.
> A concise but very accurate historical overview of existential-phenomenological perspectives in psychiatry and psychotherapy.

Macquarrie, J. (1986). *Existentialism: an introduction, guide and assessment.* Harmondsworth: Penguin.
> A very clear introduction to existentialism, which presents the ideas thematically rather than by philosopher.

Warnock, M. (1970). *Existentialism.* Oxford: Oxford University Press.
> A classic brief introduction to existentialism. There is a strong focus on Sartre and a rather pessimistic take on the future of existentialism, but this is a standard that is definitely worth reading.

FOUR   Fundamentals of Existential Practice

CHAPTER AIMS

This chapter aims to:

- provide an introduction to the fundamentals of existential therapeutic practice;
- discuss the scepticism of diagnosis and psycho-pathology of existential therapists;
- outline the practical basics for existential therapy, including the therapeutic setting and style and phases of therapy;
- discuss the use of existential therapy with couples and groups.

In this chapter I move on to consider some of the practicalities in working as an existential therapist. In many ways this chapter is the essential companion to the five chapters that follow, in which I build on the basics of existentialism outlined previously and highlight key existential concepts and their implications for practice. A beginning therapist will, of course, need to read more on the basic practicalities of working as a counsellor or psychotherapist and there are many good books which cover such things (which tutors on counselling and psychotherapy courses will recommend). Below I outline some key practical features that are specific to existential therapy that all trainees and experienced practitioners should understand. First, however, I briefly discuss the qualities needed to become an existential therapist in the hope that all those thinking of training in this therapeutic modality will reflect on their own suitability to become an existential therapist, for it is not for everyone.

Qualities needed to become an existential therapist

Deurzen-Smith (1996) distinguishes four elements necessary to become an effective existential therapist: life experience, attitude and personality, theoretical knowledge, professional training. For me, two qualities are essential for anyone wishing to train and practise as an existential therapist. The first is an open-minded attitude or perhaps this should be phrased differently, in the light of the foregoing discussion, as an ability to adopt a phenomeno-logical attitude. In a sense this is equivalent to the description of life experi-ence combined with attitude and personality by Deurzen-Smith, though is perhaps broader still since any amount of life experience does not necessar-ily lead to insight into the provisional nature of one's own beliefs and the consequent ability to stand back from these when adopting a phenomeno-logical attitude. Whilst life experience is undoubtedly valuable in confront-ing us all with the challenges of life and difference, it is how we respond to this experience – the quality of it for us personally – that is most important for a therapist. Similarly, we are not always the best judge of our capacity to set aside our beliefs. So often people believe they are able to work phe-nomenologically but in reality are simply projecting their own subjectivity onto a client. Personal therapy and feedback (via teaching and supervision) in training (and continuing throughout one's career) is crucial here for ensuring that all therapists are continually forced to face the extent of their ability to stand back from their own world view and attempt to see the world from another's perspective.

The second key element for any existential therapist is the intellectual capacity to understand, and then translate into therapeutic practice, the philosophy underpinning this particular perspective. This is akin to Deurzen-Smith's requirement for theoretical knowledge but, once again, more than this through the requirement to have the capacity to understand and translate this knowledge into practice. For me, there is a need if one is to work effectively as an existential therapist for more than a basic under-standing of philosophy. This approach is inherently philosophical and as such poses demanding intellectual challenges for the therapist, and effec-tive therapists need to have the intellectual capacity to meet such chal-lenges if they are to be able to grasp the heart of the existential way of working and then embody this in practice with their clients. Having the personal capacity to fulfil both criteria is no mean feat and one which many will struggle to achieve. Indeed, as Deurzen-Smith (1996: 183) states: 'The criteria of what makes for a good existential therapist are so high that the chances of finding bad existential therapists must be considerable.' It is the duty of all of us involved in the training of existential therapists, there-fore, to re-double our efforts to ensure that those people who leave training programmes are in a position to offer therapy of a suitable standard and to not be afraid of failing those trainees who cannot meet such a standard, should they not have gained sufficient personal insight to know that this form of therapy is not for them and left voluntarily.

Client suitability, presenting concerns and change

To some extent there are no restrictions on who might benefit from existential therapy. The history of the approach – with the work of Binswanger, Boss and Laing, to name but three – is testament to the capacity for existential therapists to engage with clients from a very wide variety of backgrounds and with very different presenting concerns. However, in general most people working as existential therapists will encounter everyday problems in living: fear, anxiety, sadness, loss and so on. These presenting concerns are very much the stuff of existential therapy and form the core of work for most people working from this perspective. This approach is particularly appropriate for people experiencing change or crises in life, people at the edge of existence or those that feel disenfranchised in some way. It is also most suitable for people who wish to question their values and assumptions and are willing to engage seriously in such work. Deurzen-Smith (1996) suggests that people who simply want symptom relief, rather than an investigation into the meaning of what concerns them, are better off being referred elsewhere. There is undoubtedly some truth in this assertion, but even amongst such people there may be possibilities for the existential therapist to work constructively to enable them to find an alternative route around their problem, if there is some willingness to explore this from the client. For me the most important issue is whether the individual therapist has both the necessary specialist knowledge and personal capacity to work with any individual client. It is not the role of the client to educate the therapist; we must do that ourselves through our ongoing professional development. It is also not appropriate for a therapist to engage a client who they do not feel comfortable working with. We all have different strengths and weaknesses and it is our personal and professional responsibility to acknowledge these, work on them, but fundamentally to recognise what is best for any (potential) client and refer on to others where appropriate.

Change is an inevitable part of life, though for many clients it is change that forms the centre of their struggle. Whilst many people freely express a desire for change, the detail of their life often reveals how they are stubbornly clinging on to the status quo. A key aspect of existential therapy is to work phenomenologically to highlight this paradox, to shine light onto the ways in which people act against their own best interests. Existential therapy is an insight-oriented therapy with the key goal for clients being greater knowledge and understanding of their lives and the realisation of their capacity to effect change in their world. For many this requires a move from objectivity to subjectivity, a move to inwardness in Kierkegaard's terms. With this move comes a more deliberate way of living, in which we acknowledge our choices and – in spite of the anxiety that this produces – face them head-on with passion. This is not easy and will also not necessarily be right for all people, but when clients do present with a desire to live differently this will inevitably form the basis for effecting change.

Diagnosis and critical psycho-pathology

Existential therapists do not readily work with notions of diagnosis and psycho-pathology. In some settings it may, of course, be unavoidable and here existential therapists will have to be particularly creative in how they deal with such demands. For most existential therapists, however, there will be a degree of flexibility around such issues and the norm will be to resist employing methods of diagnosis, such as the *Diagnostic and Statistical Manual of the American Psychiatric Association* (DSM-IV TR) or the *International Classification of Diseases* (ICD-10) from the World Health Organisation. This can be a challenge as many diagnostic labels are now part of everyday discourse. 'Depression' and 'anxiety', for instance, have become commonplace terms for describing everyday issues that we all must face but they do more than simply describe our emotional state. Such labels can undoubtedly be helpful in accessing services and avoiding pressures in life that may be experienced. They can also be helpful in garnering support from others. Telling someone we are 'depressed' is more likely to elicit a helping response than saying we are 'sad'. This is, in itself, a sad state of affairs but reflects the socio-cultural landscape of life in the West, at least, for many of us today.

It is important to explain why diagnosis and psycho-pathology are avoided by most existential therapists. The philosophical underpinnings of the approach provide the answer quite clearly. First and foremost, any notion of diagnosis does not make sense when adopting a phenomenological perspective for the focus here must, of course, be on the things in their appearing for the client. Diagnostic labels preclude this possibility because using them means that we are looking at the experience of the client using pre-determined ways of understanding what it means. This shuts down the possibility of understanding the client's experience in their own terms and instead involves the importation of an external theoretical framework. Beyond this, the existential emphasis on the uniqueness of being for each person (or more correctly, Dasein) also stresses the need to consider each person's situation as a distinct occurrence rather than as another category of pathology.

Beyond these fundamental philosophical objections to diagnosis and psycho-pathology a number of writers, notably Thomas Szasz (1961), working broadly within the existential tradition have levelled serious criticisms against the notion of psycho-pathology in general. Szasz argues that mental illnesses do not fit the criteria for physical illnesses and so should not be treated within a modified version of the traditional (physical) disease model, as they are in the psychiatric diagnostic manuals, for instance. Instead he argues that 'mental illnesses' are metaphors for problems in living and are more properly the province of moral and social choices than medical (pathologising) ones. This view is persuasive and certainly captures the spirit of many objections to the medical dominance of psychology, but there are flaws in the arguments being made and alternative positions which require serious attention (see Bowers, 1998, for a good discussion of these issues). It is very easy to draw on an argument which supports one's own position without really thinking through the logic of the argument or the evidence being employed to support it. Something as serious (for those that it concerns directly) as the use (or not) of diagnosis within the 'psy-sciences' (psychiatry, psychology and psychotherapy) requires serious thought before rushing too readily to a conclusion one way or the other.

R. D. Laing's work and writing (1960, 1961, 1967) is also worth examining in a little more detail as it continues to exert an influence on existential counselling and psychotherapy today. His critical, phenomenologically informed and compassionate take on psycho-pathology with people who were experiencing serious disturbances continues to inspire many to adopt similar strategies. Whilst attempting to understand the experience of people suffering from what is classically labelled 'schizophrenia', Laing developed the concept of *ontological insecurity*, a fundamental lack of trust in one's concrete (physical) existence in the world. Laing (ibid.) thought that such a fundamental rupture of a person's being-in-the-world led to deep anxieties which he associated with the experience of schizophrenia. Schizophrenia emerges through three threats that may follow from this insecurity: engulfment, implosion and petrification. *Engulfment* is the terror of being taken over by another, overwhelmed by the certainty of the other and their presence. *Implosion* concerns the sense of profound inner emptiness and the threat of this being filled by the other. Finally, *petrification* is where one switches off and disconnects, as if a stone and is thus depersonalised. These threats that may follow from ontological insecurity clearly describe elements of the experience of schizophrenia but, as Deurzen (1998) points out, should not only be associated with schizophrenia. For her, Laing overemphasised the link with schizophrenia and failed to recognise the way that ontic insecurity (as she argues it should be properly called) is fundamental to us all and describes the deep anxiety we can all feel when confronted with the emptiness of existence. These concepts can thus be seen as possible moments in all our lives and are therefore useful concepts for existential therapists working with clients facing a variety of dilemmas.

Laing's influence on the development of British existential therapy was undoubtedly considerable, though it is difficult to pin down his approach. It was a curious blend of existentialism and object-relational psychoanalysis, and this has resulted in no clear therapeutic legacy in his name. Laing and Cooper, his colleague, developed the Philadelphia Association, a therapeutic community which was initially run on the basis of Laing and Cooper's critical approach to psychiatry (influenced by phenomenology and existentialism). The Philadelphia Association still exists today but is now much more influenced by psychoanalytic theory, though it still maintains a broadly phenomenological focus concerning mental health and illness. The Arbours Association, another therapeutic community network, also grew out of the early work of Laing and Cooper in the 1960s and continues to this day but with a strong emphasis on Kleinian psychoanalysis. Perhaps the most significant influence has been through Emmy van Deurzen, who was attracted to the UK on the basis of Laing's work (Deurzen, 1998). Deurzen established the two main training schools for existential therapy in the UK (the School of Psychotherapy and Counselling at Regent's College and the New School of Psychotherapy and Counselling in London) along with the

Society for Existential Analysis (www.existentialanalysis.co.uk). These developments have established the UK as one of the most dynamic and important training centres for existential therapy in Europe.

The therapeutic setting

It is, of course, necessary for any therapy to have an appropriate setting. This invariably involves a room that is quiet and relatively free from disturbance, which is also comfortable so that both therapist and client can concentrate on the task at hand. I have seen clients in formal organisational therapy settings and at home, and the feel can be quite different. The home environment is more intimate and this can be a challenge for some clients and therapists alike. Clients who see a therapist in their own home will come to know more about the therapist and some therapists feel uncomfortable about this. A sense of openness, however, is a valuable quality for an existential therapist, and it would be useful to examine such anxieties about disclosure should they arise. To a great extent it is necessary to work with whatever setting is available to you as long as you feel comfortable working in it. If the therapist is not comfortable then the client is unlikely to feel secure enough to engage fully in the therapeutic process. Disturbances in the therapeutic setting are generally to be avoided but as Deurzen-Smith (1996) points out, these can also present opportunities for the existential therapist to not only model appropriate behaviour but also to reaffirm their commitment to the client by prioritising their needs over that of the disturbance.

Whilst existential therapy, like therapy of all kinds, has inherited much about the setting from psychoanalysis with an emphasis on a secure and stable frame (with consistency in meeting times, length of sessions, continued similarity of environment and so on) it is within the spirit of existential therapy to adapt this frame as appropriate. It is important not to ignore the need for consistency, but there are moments when one might consider meeting the needs of different clients in somewhat different ways. This must to be done with caution and considerable thought about the need of the client, however. The history of abuse of the frame by figures such as the (in)famous psychoanalyst Jacques Lacan, who would shorten or lengthen sessions as he saw fit often leaving clients confused and distressed, is testament to the need for consistency and care in therapy (see Grant, 2000, for a savage but rather wonderful attack on his work by Raymond Tallis). The choice between using chairs or a couch, for instance, is one example where I have worked flexibly. In general I find the use of chairs with client and therapist facing one another (though able to turn away when wanted) most productive. We are both in the same position, dealing with each other in an adult-to-adult manner. On occasions, however, the use of a couch for the client has proven to be efficacious. With clients who are very concerned with appearance (in the broadest sense), who struggle to face the therapist, meet their gaze and communicate their pain, a couch can be useful, at least in the early stages, in enabling them to talk more freely. Similarly, I have used techniques (such as the empty chair technique from Gestalt therapy) when appropriate. This does not form part of my normal way of working but on occasion I have found such things to be useful for enabling clients to better express their experience. Playing around or flagrantly ignoring knowledge gained from 100 years of therapeutic practice must be avoided at all cost but considered changes to accepted practice on a case-by-case, moment-by-moment basis are certainly within the spirit of existential therapy.

Contract

Formal contracts detailing fees, cancellation policies and endings are becoming increasingly common for therapists working in all settings. Whilst this may be in writing, and there are clear benefits to this, many therapists working in private practice do not do this so formally but instead are clear about their policies in an early session. Existential therapists seek to develop a relationship which is open and honest and as such it is important to be clear about the nature of what is being offered. Fee charges and cancellation issues are probably one of the most vexing issues for newly qualified therapists in private practice. It is important not to undervalue yourself as this may lead to resentment, but it is also important not to price yourself out of the local market. By looking around at the fees of other similarly qualified therapists it should be possible to determine an appropriate fee. It is important to think carefully about the balance of income and expenditure to avoid losing money – surprisingly easy to do when one factors in the cost of accommodation, supervision costs, professional fees and insurance, continuing professional development and so on. Many therapists like to offer low-cost therapy to those on limited incomes, and also to trainee therapists. Whilst this is undoubtedly a valuable thing to do, and is very much in the spirit of equality that is at the heart of the existential perspective, it is vital to think through the details of such arrangements if you are going to offer this option. For instance, it is generally a bad idea to give a prime session slot (e.g. 6 p.m. on a weekday) to a low-cost client or to agree to unlimited open-ended therapy with a low-cost client. Assuming the therapist needs the income to live on, then these sorts of arrangements are likely to prove problematic in the long run. It is also worth being mindful of how may trainee therapists one wishes to take on. Whilst I treat therapy the same, whether with trainees or not (though I am often more willing to engage in discussion about theory and practice with trainees), there is often a different feel when the person is attending as a course requirement rather than due to some immediate presenting concern. This can lead to an unbalanced practice, which may not prove satisfying or conducive to one's continuing professional development. Cancellation policies vary from one therapist to another but is generally fairly flexible amongst existential therapists. I ask for one day's notice if possible, but even where this is not given I rarely pursue a client for the fee. The exception, for me, is a client cancelling on the day shortly before the session, where I do expect to be recompensed. Repeated cancellations will clearly need to be addressed directly, for both practical (financial) and therapeutic reasons. That is, whilst I would not interpret repeated cancellations as a psychoanalyst might, it still provides valuable information about the way a client engages in the world that may be useful, if reflected upon and discussed, within the therapeutic process.

Ethics

Comprehensive guidelines on ethics are published by such bodies as the British Association for Counselling and Psychotherapy (BACP), the United Kingdom Council for Psychotherapy (UKCP) and the The British Psychological Society (BPS) (available on their respective websites). In general, there are a number of key principles which underpin most ethical standards including:

- **Fidelity:** honouring the trust placed in the practitioner.
- **Autonomy:** respect for the client's right to be self-governing.
- **Beneficence:** a commitment to promoting the client's well-being.
- **Non-maleficence:** a commitment to avoiding harm to the client.
- **Justice:** the fair and impartial treatment of all clients and the provision of adequate services.
- **Self-respect:** fostering the practitioner's self-knowledge and care for self.

These principles from the BACP exemplify the spirit of ethical existential practice and should be concepts that are familiar to all therapists, whatever their theoretical orientation. Existential therapy seeks to work in a non-judgemental way through the phenomenological method to enable clients to gain greater mastery of themselves and, therefore, greater autonomy. This theoretical principle is directly aligned with an ethics in which beneficence and justice are key. Of course, these principles may at times come into conflict with each other, and that speaks to the heart of ethical decision-making: all practitioners must draw on such principles and their knowledge/experience to determine what is ethically appropriate for themselves. There have been attempts to provide guidance on how this might be determined (see, for instance, Bond, 2009), but ultimately ethical decisions are made by the practitioner (often in consultation with a supervisor or experienced colleague) on a case-by-case basis. The major caveat to this is that if one is a member of a professional body (such as the BACP, UKCP or BPS), then it is vital that they are aware of the professional body ethical guidelines/standards and adhere to them in their work. Existential therapists are likely to be a member of one of these organisations and should, therefore, abide by the principles of their governing body. Tim Bond's (2009) book *Standards and Ethics for Counselling in Action* is a standard text which is well worth consulting for more on these issues.

Therapeutic style

Existential therapists differ somewhat in their therapeutic style, with some assuming the relative quiet of the psychoanalyst whilst others are more engaged and talkative. There is no hard-and-fast rule about which is best, though for me the spirit of existential therapy suggests a more conversational style. But we are not talking about a chat amongst friends here so what does it mean to adopt a conversational style in therapy? The conversation we are talking about here has a clear purpose, the clarification and exploration of the client's world as it relates to their presenting concerns; it is not a conversation about the therapist and their views, beliefs or concerns. In the process of exploring the client's world the therapist will need to ensure that they have grasped the meaning of what is being said, and this will necessarily require that they ask for concrete examples of whatever is being discussed: to work phenomenologically it is essential that there are concrete examples of the experiences being recounted. Clarification throughout will be necessary, alongside questions about the meaning of things being discussed. In addition, it will be appropriate to ask questions and pose challenges to a client. By drawing on the work of the existentialists a therapist will begin to have questions about the assumptions and values of a client, the ways in which they have constructed their account and how this particular way of engaging in the world both allows and limits their possibilities. The conversation is therefore akin to a philosophical dialogue with the therapist as 'tutor in the art of living' (Deurzen-Smith, 1997). That does not mean they are the 'expert in the art of living' but rather trained to provide guidance in how a client might come to live their life better, in their own terms which is not necessarily the same as the terms of the therapist.

In the early stages of the therapy the existential therapist will be working carefully to encourage the client to describe their world and so will probably be relatively quiet, asking for more detail, more examples and clarification about the meaning of what is being recounted. With the groundwork established within a supportive therapeutic relationship, however, an existential therapist may take the opportunity to question more readily and to challenge where appropriate. This is not through argument but rather through interventions designed to highlight aspects of the client's world that were previously not attended to, aspects that were either disavowed or out of immediate awareness. Clients need to be encouraged to do much of this work themselves, for interventions will likely only have real meaning when the client is ready to hear them. The client therefore needs to be encouraged to adopt the phenomenological attitude – not through an explicit discussion of the philosophy, but through the actions of the therapist in asking for detail, in exploring the minutiae of the issues and in refraining from any moves beyond the things in their appearing. A key element of this process is pattern recognition, with the therapist acting as the memory bank for all of the therapeutic work, across all sessions, able to spot emerging patterns in the way the client is making sense of their world. This pattern recognition exercise will, of course, be informed by the philosophy underpinning practice and so will be relational, with both parties seeking to work together, and hermeneutic, designed to open up new ways of understanding.

A therapist will need to adapt their style to meet the needs of different clients. This is not about compromising the methods of existential therapy but instead of embodying them subtly with care for the way in which each client relates differently. Some clients will need much more engagement and support early on, with much more friendly chat to enable them to feel safe enough to reveal details about their troubles, whilst others will need more silence and space to think through their problems. As with any therapy the good therapist needs to tune in to the style of the client and not just follow their own style of working regardless. But this is not simply a case of moving towards and meeting a client's needs as required, for any such move reveals something about the being-in-the-world of the client and so provides us with insight into their way of relating with others. Part of the process of therapy involves the therapist in noting the way a client relates and potentially offering an alternative way of relating through the course of the therapy, either through questioning and challenging or through gradually shifting and modelling a different way of being in a relationship with another person.

Phases of therapeutic engagement

Spinelli (2007) outlines three phases in working with clients as an existential therapist, which in general provide a useful guide for all existential therapists when working long-term or in an open-ended way with clients.[1] Indeed, to some extent these three phases are similar to the different elements of therapy described by Deurzen (2002) and are recognisable in my own work also. There are differences in the detail of what might be contained within these three stages between my own work (and, I suspect, Deurzen's) and that of Spinelli, but there are some overarching similarities that are worth discussing here. To a certain extent these three phases

---

[1]Short-term work will, of course, require a more flexible way of working. This often involves the therapist working more directly with the client in activities that might be described as Stage 2 in Spinelli's three phases.

simply represent the beginning, middle and end of therapy, though Spinelli (ibid.) describes them as: co-creating the therapy world, exploring the therapy world, and closing down the therapy world.

The first phase represents the beginning of any therapeutic encounter and for Spinelli (ibid.) is the time in which the therapist and client co-create the 'therapy world'. This includes setting the frame for therapy, where boundaries are made clear and respected, the contract established and the client's world view explored within the context of the therapeutic relationship. There is flexibility about who speaks first and spontaneity as the client and therapist meet each other. In an initial meeting, however, it will be important to hear the client's story and start to get a sense of both the 'what' and 'how' (see Chapter 2) of their experience. The focus is on staying with the client and attending to their experience in the phenomenological attitude. There is no judging or attempt at fixing the client but instead a steady free-floating phenomenological concern with understanding their experience, as given. This in itself is often sufficient to establish rapport and a good working relationship, but it may also be necessary with some clients to go further to meet their needs and where appropriate provide support and encouragement in this early phase. Deurzen (2002) highlights the central role of anxiety present in the early stages of therapy and this must be handled with care. Some clients will be able to sustain this anxiety with little assistance from the therapist, whilst others may need some reassurance and support to ensure that the anxiety works to energise the engagement rather than paralyse it.

The second phase of therapy occurs once a firm therapeutic relationship has been established and time spent descriptively exploring the client's world view. Here there may be more active engagement on the part of the existential therapist, with challenges offered to dispositional stances that serve to maintain the client's presenting difficulties, where appropriate. More risks are taken now that the therapeutic relationship has been established and the client better able to feed back to the therapist and challenge and correct them. This is a joint exercise with both client and therapist now able to work together more actively, offering feedback on the content and process of the therapy. For Spinelli, Deurzen and myself this phase represents the heart of the work and the point at which the therapist draws more heavily on existential philosophy to inform their interventions (see Part II).

The third stage represents the process of ending the work or the 'closing down' of the therapy world, in Spinelli's (2007) terms. Here there is a sense that the work of the therapist has been exhausted with the client now taking the lead in exploring their own world and better placed for the challenges of life. There may also be a sense that they have internalised the voice of the therapist and can carry their conversations with them beyond the therapy. Spinelli describes a bridging process where the focus shifts more to how the client can take their insights from the therapy room out into their world. This will, of course, have been explored prior to this point but becomes an acute focus as the therapy nears its conclusion. Reviewing the work, what has been learnt and the changes that have occurred for the client are valuable exercises here in enabling them to reflect on how much progress has been made. Of course, issues will still remain, as they do for us all, but clients who feel ready to leave therapy will invariably be better placed to meet these without the therapist at their side. Having a contracted number of sessions in which to end the work is often useful to gradually phase out and close down the therapy world but sometimes this is not possible (if working in a time-limited way, for instance) and then – even if the work seems incomplete – it is important to review the progress and support the client in taking what has been learnt forward themselves. Often it is the client who suggests ending the work, and this will normally represent their readiness to move on from the relationship. Occasionally, however, a client bringing up the issue of ending may represent a sense of frustration about the work. It is important, therefore, that the therapist thinks carefully about a request to end from a client. I invariably find that I too have been thinking about the end of the work when a client brings up the issue of ending, but on occasions I find myself feeling it is too early. It is not the therapist's place to keep a client in therapy, however, and whilst I may ask about their desire to end, my priority must be to respect their wishes and support them in their decision-making regardless. Some therapists become dependent on their clients, not only for the income but also for the relationship, and this must always be guarded against: we are offering a professional service that is for the client, not for ourselves.

Working with individuals, couples and groups

Most existential therapy is conducted with individuals in the typical dyadic therapeutic situation. There are many existential therapists who, however, also offer couples therapy, and a smaller number who work with groups. Most writing on existential therapy concerns individual therapy with relatively little written on working with couples and groups, and this book is no exception. This is a serious gap in the literature which needs to be addressed, but undoubtedly reflects the state of contemporary existential practice. There is not the space in this book for detailed consideration of couple or group work but below I very briefly (too briefly, in truth) discuss some of the key issues and writing on these issues for existential therapists.

Making the transition from working existentially with individuals to working with couples is relatively easy in comparison with group work, though still offers some unique challenges. In many ways the skills honed by the existential therapist working with individuals are transferable to working with couples with only a few modifications. Furthermore, the relational philosophy underpinning existential therapy, alongside standard therapeutic ideas about couple work, offers a firm ground for couple work. Couple work invariably involves the therapist engaged systematically in working with each individual to clarify the presenting concern as they see it and in the process also their world view and values. This in itself is often incredibly valuable as each member of a couple comes to understand the ways in which they have become entrenched in seeing the problem and the effect that this has had on their partner and the relationship. Finding ways for couples to better communicate their thoughts and feelings to each other is also key in enabling them to work outside the therapeutic situation to improve their situation. The therapist must attend to the relationship not only between each client and him- or herself, but also the relationship between each member of the couple and draw on the relevant philosophical ideas underpinning relationships (discussed in detail in Chapter 8) to find ways of encouraging new ways of relating.

There is a need for more active participation on the part of the therapist, acting as referee sometimes, so that both parties feel they are given sufficient space (though this may not mean that they each spend the same amount of time talking). It is also important for the therapist to stress to couples that they need to work outside the therapy if they are to effect lasting change. Too often one (or occasionally both) member(s) of a couple will expect all change to occur within the sessions and will wait for the next session before discussing anything with their partner. It would be unusual for an existential therapist working one-to-one with a client to provide 'homework' but with couples activities are often negotiated within sessions so they know what might be useful work for them to do between sessions. In a sense this is a reflection of the tendency for couple work to be shorter than one-to-one, as it is often more focussed and also limited in duration by the willingness of each member of the couple to sustain the relationship in its present form. Overall, however, the key factor in success is whether both members of the couple really want the relationship to work and are prepared to make the necessary changes to realise this outcome.

Group work has been discussed by Cohn (1997) and Tantam (2005) and this provides some insights into some of the possibilities for working in this way from an existential perspective. Cohn (ibid.) draws on the insights of group analysts (principally Foulkes) to formulate some initial suggestions for existential group work, drawing further on Heidegger, which I outline here. Group work, in Heideggerian terms, is arguably the most appropriate setting for psychotherapy for it is here that there is the real possibility for working with the relational foundation of Dasein, rather than abstracting the individual from this context. Psychological disturbances therefore become disturbances of relationality and communication within the group provides the means by which such disturbances can be observed and addressed directly. In line with the principles of group analysis, the therapist in an existential group should see him- or herself as part of the group (not above it or outside it) and should act accordingly, communicating their own understandings and feelings to the group process as appropriate. That is not to say that the therapist offers the same as all the other group members in terms of personal disclosure but rather that they do not attempt to hide from the group by acting as some objective observer of events. Working through past relationships in the group (transference relationships in psychoanalytic terms) represent the multi-dimensionality of time with the past and future always inflected in the present and are therefore part of the business of the group, with the therapist acting to enable the group to work through the meaning of such events. Finally, Cohn (ibid.) argues that all material discussed in the group relating to what occurs outside the group is relevant and part of the material of the group (unlike some forms of group analysis which separate what is inside and outside the group and consider that only that which occurs in the group is relevant).

Tantam (2005) draws on a variety of work to explore the implications of group work for existential therapy. He first explores the tension between groups and those existentialists that might be characterised (often unfairly) as individualistic and concerned about the loss of subjectivity that occurs through membership of groups and also wider society. Following this, he mentions briefly the later work of Sartre (1960/2004) and his *Critique of Dialectical Reason*, along with other work by more contemporary psychologists of group functions and processes. Two key elements that Tantam explores for existential groups are anxiety and dialogue. Although these are dealt with very briefly they are clearly important topics for existential group analysts to consider in their work. Anxiety has many effects on groups and feelings of 'homelessness' (*unheimlichkeit* in Heidegger's terms) may offer clues about the way a person is experiencing the group in a new way through a sense of alienation that comes about when cut off from the group norms. Similarly, Buberian (1923/1958) notions of dialogue and relating (discussed in detail in Chapter 8) provide insight into the ways in which constructive dialogue may be a means of creating a community and resolving conflicts. This work, along with Cohn's (1997) use of Heidegger, is undoubtedly useful for beginning to formulate an existential theory of groups, but more is still needed if such group work is to develop coherently and systematically and offer something new that is informed by both existential philosophy and also the work of group analysts and psychologists.

Further reading

Bowers, L. (1998). *The social nature of mental illness*. London: Routledge.
 A comprehensive account of contemporary debates around mental illness, diagnosis and psycho-pathology. I do not agree with all of the author's arguments, but it is very much worth reading.

Spinelli, E. (2007). *Practising existential psychotherapy: the relational world.* London: Sage.

> A very clear account of Spinelli's approach to the practice of existential therapy. The chapters concerning the three phases of therapy are of particular note.

Deurzen, E. van (2002). *Existential counselling and psychotherapy in practice.* London: Sage.

> A very clear account of Deurzen's approach to the practice of existential therapy. It forms a useful companion text to *Everyday Mysteries*, Deurzen-Smith's (1997) other main book on existential therapy.

Part II

Developing Existential Therapy

Part II

FIVE   Anxiety – The Core of Existence

CHAPTER AIMS

This chapter aims to:

- provide an introduction to a number of key ideas central to existential therapeutic practice including: anxiety, eternal recurrence and *amor fati*, and authenticity and being-towards-death;
- explain how these philosophical concepts can be applied in practice;
- use a number of case studies to show the value of these concepts in different situations.

This chapter and those that follow in this Part provide coverage of a number of key philosophical concepts and their application within existential therapy. Existential therapy is not simply a ragbag of philosophical ideas thrown at clients and the chapters in this Part should be seen as building on the ideas and methods already outlined. As I mentioned at the very beginning of the book, existential therapy uses the phenomenological method first and foremost and then incorporates ideas from existentialism (and hermeneutics, discussed in Chapter 11) to further understand what is going on for a client when they come to see us. The fundamentals of existential thought were discussed in the previous chapter and some ideas will be revisited here with more of a focus on practice than previously. In addition, the following chapters introduce ideas from a number of other existential philosophers including Sartre, Merleau-Ponty and others. The key with all of these ideas is that they must not be seen as discrete concepts or – even worse – techniques but ways of deepening our understanding of the human condition for ourselves and our clients. Good existential practice involves the therapist embodying the ideas contained in this book (and probably others) and then acting as translator, using them hermeneutically to enable the client to open up new possibilities for how they understand their life. In order to become an effective existential therapist it is also vital that we too engage with this philosophy in a practical manner, to examine our own lives and continually work to live them with due respect to the unique privilege of existence.

In both this and the following chapters some of these ideas will be given much more space than others. This may reflect the fact that some have been covered already (at least in part) in the previous chapters and that some demand greater explanation and warrant more attention as they are more fundamental to therapy. The order of the concepts presented is not arbitrary but generally reflects their historical emergence in the existential literature. This chapter focuses on anxiety and external recurrence as ideas emerging from the roots of existential philosophy (and the work of Kierkegaard and Nietzsche), though also addressed later by other thinkers. Authenticity and being-towards-death have already been introduced in the section on Heidegger but will be revisited here, albeit briefly, with a focus on practice, due to their link with the overriding theme of this chapter. The central theme throughout this chapter is the finite quality of life. Human awareness of our being-towards-death produces anxiety, which provides the vital force for existence, realised through authentic living, though may also, of course, be crippling. One consequence of such an awareness is the need to live life to the maximum, with passion, and it is here that Nietzsche's ideas about eternal recurrence and *amor fati* are crucial for understanding how this might be realised.

Anxiety

Existential anxiety (or more properly, angst) has already been introduced in the previous chapter when discussing the work of Kierkegaard and Heidegger. For Kierkegaard, angst is the price we pay for freedom, when we free ourselves from the shackles of objectivity and live in inwardness. Whilst angst is translated into English as 'anxiety', this does not have the same meaning as specific anxieties, such as the anxiety we may feel when giving a talk or meeting new people: anxiety in this existential sense is ontological and a universal part of existence. Our ontic experiences of anxiety may, however, provide an insight into the way we are facing the world (our mood or 'attunement', in Heidegger's terms) and is a manifestation of our ontological angst. Cohn (1997: 70), drawing predominantly on Heidegger, explains that our angst stems from:

- our *thrownness* into a world we did not choose (e.g. the time and place, our body and so on);
- the necessity to make choices (and even to make no choice is a choice), the outcomes of which are never certain and always imply the rejection of alternatives;
- the realisation that life is inevitably moving towards death.

Life discloses itself to us through anxiety as this highlights those moments when our freedom and finitude become apparent. This is different from fear, which has a particular target and is a secondary emotion to anxiety. Yalom (1980) drew on these ideas to propose two defences against such anxiety: the *I am special* defence and the *ultimate rescuer* defence. The *I am special* defence concerns the way in which some people convince themselves that they are special in order to protect themselves against the threat of death. By working up a sense of their own importance, their unique contribution to life, they make themselves feel invaluable and not just one of many. In many ways we all do this to some extent but Yalom is highlighting people for whom this becomes destructive, as they may engage in excessive risk-taking (demonstrating their invulnerability) or aggression. This can be seen in extreme workaholism, where a person loses sight of the range of possibilities available to them in life and concentrates exclusively on one aspect of their being, making themselves feel special. Not only can this lead to dissatisfaction when reflected upon, but it can also leave considerable destruction in its wake as other people are forgotten in the pursuit of this goal. The *ultimate rescuer* defence is where a person has a belief that someone or something will rescue them from the inevitability of death. This may involve some fundamentalist religious belief where the person ignores their own agency and individual moral duty or the belief that some other figure (a parent or even therapist) will save them.

Deurzen (2002) highlights how the beginning of all therapy is likely to involve anxiety and that this ontic manifestation is revealing of aspects of being. The way a client deals with the initial anxiety generated by visiting a therapist is likely to be a good indicator of the way that they face anxiety more generally in life. A person who appears to be mindlessly engaged in life, talking in therapy endlessly about the trivialities of their everyday experience, tells us something about the way they are (potentially, for all such understandings must be contingent and grounded in the experience with any individual client) protecting themselves from the anxiety of a more passionate (inward facing) engagement in life, and also therapy. Similarly, the apathetic client who looks to the therapist for solutions to their problems is likely to act in this way in other aspects of their life. The role of the existential therapist is to work phenomenologically to understand what is being revealed, and through this process build the relationship and the trust that is necessary for further work to take place.

Once the ground has been established in this way it becomes possible to begin to work with the client to challenge their taken-for-granted assumptions about the world, to question whether they are acting in their own best interests, and to encourage them to open up their world through an increased preparedness to face the anxiety that living passionately inevitably entails. Anxiety in these terms, then, is not something that should be lessened (through some sense of cure) but used creatively – as it highlights what is being closed down in the world – to provide the drive to engage in the world differently. Of course, some clients will be overcome by anxiety and care must be taken to provide the necessary support for such clients to find ways of dealing with their anxiety. This must not be a case of the therapist providing answers or blindly pushing clients into activities that they do not feel ready to face but a working together in full recognition of the power of anxiety so that the client can find their own route through their struggle.

Case study Carol and the struggle with anxiety

Carol is 61 and married, for the second time, to Bert. She came to therapy as a result of her feeling out of control with her fears. She worried continually about her husband and his health and her sons and their well-being. This had become increasingly problematic as Carol now refused to go overseas on holiday, for fear that something might happen to Bert and she find herself alone. She also found herself engaged with her older son in an overly protective way that added to her stress and anxiety. Carol had considerable insight and recognised very early on that the death of her mother, whom she was very close to, had led to an increase in her anxieties around the other members of her family. Her anxiety did, however, pre-date the death of her mother and she recognised that she 'had always been an anxious person'. Carol visited a counsellor prior to seeing me who she thought was 'not much cop'. I was aware that whilst Carol seemed to disclose a great deal early on that it would take some time to gain her trust in me. There was also a gendered dimension to this with Carol apparently more ready to trust a man (in what she perceived as a professional position of responsibility) than a woman, which was advantageous in the short-term for me in developing trust in the relationship but potentially something for us to explore at a later date should she wish to do so.

Later in this first phase of therapy I gently tested out my ability to challenge Carol with a few questions about her ability to act differently and confront her fears, and it became apparent that this was too much for her at this time. She would readily break down in tears and cry 'I know I am useless but can't do anything else'. I focused on staying with her experience and working to identify her strengths, especially concerning her ability to confront other aspects of her anxiety. Leaving her first husband was one such example which demonstrated her capacity to confront her anxiety (of throwing her comfortable life up in the air) and sustain her anxiety in an ultimately productive way for her. This move had, however, also contributed to her need for a firm foundation and fear of loss. In time we were able to address the loss of her mother, her over-concerned relationship with her son and her general anxiety towards life. There were many tears but I felt this time she was able to work through it. She remained someone who described herself as anxious at the end of our work but by confronting it more readily in the therapeutic setting felt better able to make choices that raised her anxiety levels when she felt they were worth it. This was only a relatively small step, but resulted in Carol feeling more able to live her life with her husband in a way that was satisfying to them both. I wonder about the future impact of loss on Carol but this must remain unknown to us both, for now at least.

Eternal recurrence and *amor fati*

These two concepts come from the work of Nietzsche (1908/1979), with eternal recurrence briefly introduced in the previous chapter. *Eternal recurrence* is a concept that, if embraced, not only acts as a marker for good mental health but is also a clue for how to live well. Eternal recurrence is effectively a thought experiment where we imagine living our lives again and again, making the same decisions with the same outcomes for all eternity. If we think of our lives and test them against this criteria, how do they measure up? Are we sufficiently satisfied that we have faced the world with courage and made the right decisions or have we simply followed the crowd? Are there things we wanted to do but never got around to it, or decisions we were too scared to make? Yalom (2005: 251), in his fictionalised account of the meeting of Nietzsche and Josef Breuer, describes it thus:

> [E]ternal recurrence means that every time you choose an action you must be willing to choose it *for all eternity*. And it is the same for every action, *not* made, every stillborn thought, every choice avoided. And all unlived life will remain bulging inside you, unlived through all eternity. And the unheeded voice of your conscience will cry out to you forever … *Do you hate the idea? Or do you love it? … live in such a way that you love the idea.*

And so was born the concept of *amor fati*, where Nietzsche calls to us to love our fate, to live in such a way that we embrace our choices in life and learn to accept the hand that we have been dealt and make the best of it for ourselves, in our own terms and not those of others. These are powerful rallying calls for us to examine our lives such that we live them knowingly, such that we make choices that fulfil us even when they fill us with terror. The danger for Nietzsche is living an unexamined life, a life as part of the herd, following blindly what is expected of us and then looking back with regret at choices we have made or not made. This missionary spirit represents the heart of existentialism, being a practical philosophy that if heeded provides insights into how we might better live our lives.

In therapy these ideas can operate in two ways: as concepts the therapist can draw upon to inform our understanding of the client, and as direct challenges to the client. More often it will be the former, where we work with our clients to examine their lives together and in the process offer up questions and challenges which reflect the need to find ways of living, in their own terms, that they find fulfilling. This might simply be a question about whether a client must remain in their current situation or a challenge when they say they have no choice ('is that true that it must always be this way?'). Although occasionally we might just choose to employ this thought experiment directly, with clients who would engage with both the intellectual and the emotional quality of the idea, as a way of highlighting their current predicament. Such a method needs to be used with caution as clients cannot, and should not, be browbeaten into living differently but must discover this for themselves should they have the will to do so. This subtlety in application is often missed by beginning existential therapists who get caught up in the missionary zeal of the existential movement but is key here, as elsewhere, if such interventions are going to enable clients to shift and grow. We may often leap ahead but only rarely should we leap in for our clients (Heidegger, 1927/1962); they must come to understand and make choices themselves, in their own terms and in their own time.

Case study   Joseph and his diagnosis

Joseph is 30 years old, gay and recently single. He came to see me following an instance of unsafe sex about his fears that he might have been infected with HIV. He was clearly extremely distressed at the prospect of becoming HIV positive, with very high levels of anxiety attached to his generalised fear of being alone (exacerbated by recently breaking up with his partner of six years). The early sessions involved support and also some education when appropriate about routes of infection and treatment options. There was a twin focus on addressing his affective state and also cognitive aspects of his fear. This worked, to some extent, to help him gather himself a little more to face the outcome of his HIV test. Unfortunately for Joseph, his test proved positive and his mood became increasingly depressed. He could not see a way to live, believing that this inevitably meant he would be alone forever. The positive diagnosis, for him, marked a break in his lifeworld, a rupture in his story of selfhood such that what he hoped for in the past could no longer be achieved. He could not accept the diagnosis and turned inward, rejecting any social support from friends and became increasingly isolated. I needed to work gently with him during this time, focussing on providing the support he so desperately needed. With time, however, he demonstrated a greater capacity to reflect on his situation and talk more openly about it, and this became an opportunity for me to gently help him to find ways of learning to accept his fate (*amor fati*). This involved us in discussions about both practical moves he could make (joining a support group for men living with HIV) and also challenging his belief that living with HIV inevitably meant living alone. This was a long process and not one that could or should be rushed, and with such a challenge to a person's sense of selfhood any notion of *amor fati* needed to be handled with considerable care. A rash or thoughtless intervention suggesting that he should learn to embrace his fate would have only led to distance between us and him feeling even more alone. But with gentle handling and considerable time, it was possible to introduce this concept within our work in a way that was supportive and encouraging.

Authenticity and being-towards-death

Authenticity is a key concept in Heidegger's (1927/1962) work that was discussed in Chapter 4 in some detail. As I pointed out there, it is frequently misunderstood to be some goal for living in which we live true to ourselves. Living as part of *the they* is a fundamental state for Dasein, as a result of Dasein *falling* – another term from Heidegger (ibid.), which refers to the movement of everyday being-in-the-world. Polt (1999) uses the example of someone browsing the magazine shelves of a newsagent, glancing at the different covers and skimming through the magazines, casually taking in the gossip and news in a superficial manner such that time passes without notice, and then we find ourselves jolted back into existence when we remember why we went to the shop in the first place. There is a sense of wasted time and no depth in what has been accomplished. Heidegger argues that life is like this, with us simply fulfilling the everyday routines established by others and that this superficiality is the mainstay of existence, protecting us from the angst that comes from an awareness of our being-towards-death. We can move beyond this way of encountering the world as we become aware of the finite nature of existence and strive to live more deeply for ourselves but this will always be a temporary affair, we can never totally move beyond our fallen state but only realise moments of authenticity. We are always *thrown* into a world that pre-dates us and provides our everyday ways of living and this comfortable way of existing provides the tools through which we must make sense of life. Our fallen state therefore cannot be overcome or seen as a worse state of being for total and permanent authenticity is not possible, as we would then have no basis for our understanding of the world (which comes from the past into the present in which we are thrown).

As mentioned in the previous chapter, a variety of writers since Heidegger have suggested ways in which we might defend ourselves against the anxiety of death, with such methods as the 'I am special' or 'ultimate rescuer' defence (Yalom, 1980). Cooper and Adams (2005: 79–80) provide a comprehensive list of other possible defences (amended slightly here):

- Assuming that we will have a long life, and that death is many years off (Tillich, 1967).
- Reassuring ourselves with a 'logical' attitude towards death (Jaspers, 1932/1971): for instance, saying to ourselves that when we are dead, we will not know about it, so it does not matter. Imagining death as a peaceful and restful sleep, rather than as the complete absence of all being.
- Adopting a belief in spiritual immortality, reincarnation or an afterlife (Baumeister, 1991).
- Striving to achieve 'secular immortality' through producing something that will survive our deaths, such as children, a book or work of art (Becker, 1973; Baumeister, 1991).
- Withdrawing from close emotional or sexual contact with others, to minimize the fear of separation (Firestone, 1994).
- Dissociating from our embodied, sexual being: that part of us that is vulnerable to illness and death (Firestone, 1994).
- Adopting a frivolous, excessively cheerful attitude towards life (May, 1999); or a nonchalant, indifferent attitude (Jaspers, 1932/1971).
- Adopting a depressed, phlegmatic and helpless attitude towards life (Becker, 1973; May, 1999).

- Committing suicide as a way of taking back control from the uncertainty of death (Farber, 2000).
- Immersing ourselves in obsessions, compulsions, pseudo-problems, causes, groups and/or addictions – particularly drugs and alcohol (Firestone, 1994) – to obtain some temporary relief from the anxiety of facing death.

Whilst these all may, in Heidegger's terms, represent an attempt to flee from the anxiety of death, they should not be understood as simply poor defences adopted by those unable to face the inevitability of death, and thus closing down their worlds whilst offering a modicum of relief. Whilst this may be the case for some clients, as existential therapists we have a primary duty to work phenomenologically to ensure that we do not move away from the lifeworld towards speculative theory. If a client is content with an aspect of their world (such as their alcohol use or desire to produce a sense of immortality through work), then it is not our place to deny that. We may question but when doing so we also always need to listen to the answers and treat them with the respect they are due. For those people where these defences are problematic responses to the threat of death, with their worlds being closed down, then it may, of course, be appropriate to work with them to understand how these flight reactions are providing only temporary relief and that by embracing their courage to face the inevitable uncertainty of life they might realise a capacity for more passionate living and a better quality of life.

> **Activity**   Spend some time thinking through the everyday elements of your life and your own defences towards the anxiety of death (we all have them to some degree). Write a paragraph about whether these defences are useful or troubling for you and how you might go about changing them should this be something you wish to do. If you are in therapy then use this opportunity to explore such issues further, examining in close quarters the detail of your life in terms of authenticity and being-towards-death.

The impact of being-towards-death not only concerns authenticity but also more general issues of temporality, such as ageing. The fact that we live in time and experience this on an ontic level as a fundamental part of our everyday life is significant for many aspects of existential practice. Aside from the death of someone close to us, ageing represents the most obvious way in which our experience of time (temporality) moves from the ground of our experience into concrete awareness in our everyday life. The speed at which time passes shifts and changes through our life, and the awareness of the frailty of our bodies will inevitably become more apparent with age. Experience of illness of ourselves and others will increase with age, and social expectations about ageing, beauty and desire will also likely become more apparent. Of course, greater knowledge and wisdom may also come with age and our attitudes towards social norms may shift with beauty (re)construed in broader terms beyond that of the youthful body. The key is how we engage with the inevitability of ageing and reject or embrace social norms around ageing.

Case study Jeremy and the fear of ageing

Jeremy came to see me concerned that his life was no longer fulfilling. He was a gay man in his mid-forties who had being living a very full life, working hard to earn the money to go out with friends clubbing, having lots of casual sex with few responsibilities. He said he loved his life but found himself feeling increasingly depressed and did not know why. Jeremy had come out very early and left home 'to explore the world'. He had lived on his own for most of his life with only one or two longer-term relationships (of one year or more). These had broken up as he grew dissatisfied with the 'humdrum' quality of his life with his partner. He sought excitement and realised this most often through casual sex. Jeremy was very concerned with his appearance and spent considerable time and money on ensuring that he always looked good. He never left the house unless he felt he looked good and this sometimes resulted in him staying in the house alone when he was not feeling he looked at his best. He belittled people who did not 'look after themselves', especially those who were overweight or in his terms 'ugly'. I maintained a gentle stance with Jeremy early in our work and only later began to offer up challenges to his statements about beauty and desirability. It became clear that Jeremy held an idealised notion of beauty as the province of the young and used this ideal as his model for selfhood. Whilst this had served him well – in his own terms (for instance, in securing sexual partners easily) – for many years he was becoming increasingly aware of his own ageing process. Whilst he sought to ameliorate this through attention to his appearance and continued reassurance through attracting others the inevitability of ageing and the loss of youth could not be avoided. Our work initially focussed on challenging his notion of beauty and particularly his tendency to dismiss others who failed to live up to his particular ideal. With this, he started to be more open to other aspects of selfhood (characteristics including humour, determination and compassion) though he was reluctant to let go of the notion of beauty as everything. The focus then shifted to his own sense of self and his body. He resisted the notion of ageing and worked tirelessly to defend against this perceived threat, but in spite of this he still acknowledged the inevitability of this process. We examined how he might live his life differently, still embracing the 'fun' elements but also looking for other ways of getting a sense of self-worth. One of the key moments was his realisation that whilst the casual sex was enjoyable he really did want the intimacy of a relationship. This realisation might have been obvious to others, but Jeremy's way of living had effectively enabled him to hide it from himself. Towards the end of our work it was clear that Jeremy still held his ideals of beauty although he had started to acknowledge and value aspects of others beyond this alone. He remained committed to 'keeping his looks' but had started to look at the possibility of a relationship, and with this felt he no longer needed to see me. Although the shifts in Jeremy's outlook were small, he nevertheless felt more able to carry on with his life in a way that left him feeling more satisfied.

Further reading

Heidegger, M. (1927/1962). *Being and time* (Trans. J. Macquarrie & E. Robinson). Oxford: Blackwell.
> Probably the most important book for those wishing to become an existential therapist. It is undoubtedly very difficult, but when read in conjunction with (or after) the book by Polt it should prove immensely illuminating.

May, R. (1983). *The discovery of being*. New York: W.W. Norton.
> A classic introduction to existential therapy and many of the fundamental philosophical ideas underpinning the perspective from one of the pioneers of existential therapy in the US.

Polt, R. (1999). *Heidegger: an introduction*. London: UCL Press.
> The very best introduction to Heidegger's thought you can buy. It concentrates on 'Being and Time' and so does not include reference to the Zollikon seminars, but it is a book that should be read by every existential therapist wishing to grasp this complex body of thought.

Yalom, I. (2005). *When Nietzsche wept*. New York: Harper Collins.
> A novel by one of the leading US existential therapists, which beautifully introduces the ideas of Nietzsche through a fictional account of the meeting of Breuer (one of the founding figures of psychoanalysis) and Nietzsche. An absolute pleasure to read.

SIX   The Dimensions of Existence

CHAPTER AIMS

This chapter aims to:

- provide an introduction to the dimensions of existence, including working with dreams;
- explain how the dimensions can be applied in practice;
- use a number of case studies to show the value of these concepts in different situations.

The notion of four dimensions that comprise all human experience has not been mentioned previously but for many existential therapists forms a central part of their work. The four dimensions include: the physical, the psychological, the social and the spiritual. In this chapter I also look at working with dreams and the way Boss re-worked Freudian dream analysis to produce an existential approach to dreams. Dream analysis is included alongside the four dimensions as I consider dreams the fifth dimension, a place in which there is unfettered access to the manifestation of the four dimensions: a meta-dimension if you will. That is, through sustained engagement with a client's dreams we have the opportunity to critically examine all dimensions of their lives across the range of existential fractions of the lifeworld that underpin all existence.

The four dimensions

Binswanger (1958, 1963), in his early formulation of existential therapy, first outlined the importance of examining life through three dimensions or modes: the *umwelt*, the *mitwelt* and the *eigenwelt*. These loosely translate as the physical world (umwelt), the social world (mitwelt) and the psychological world (eigenwelt). The idea is simple though inflected with important subtleties: that there are three universal dimensions to human existence and that therapists can usefully attend to how a client might be living well (or not) in each of the three. The dimensions do, of course, overlap but this idea remains a useful one for existential therapy. Much later, Deurzen-Smith (1984, 1988) suggested that there should be a fourth dimension, the *überwelt* or spiritual dimension. One of the key elements then of existential practice is to attend to how our clients are engaged with these four dimensions of existence, whether they are in balance or one or more neglected.

Whilst the *umwelt* is now generally referred to in English as the physical dimension, the literal translation is 'world-around'. This refers to the biological or environmental aspects of existence, all the physical objects about us in the world, including the biological aspect of our own bodies. It crucially involves those aspects of existence which fall into the realm of natural law, birth and death, waking and sleeping, health and ill-health. Whilst existentialists resist any notion of life being reduced to biology (or simple models of psychology concerned with instinctual drives), this does not mean a rejection of our experience of biology or the natural world. Our existence is grounded in biology and the natural world and this is a key element in how we make sense of ourselves and others. Our sense of our bodies (embodiment) is central from the moment of birth until death and the focus on the physical dimension that Binswanger alerts us to has its history in the early existential work of Kierkegaard and Nietzsche. Both Kierkegaard and Nietzsche took the body seriously and recognised that consciousness cannot be separated, as if a ghost in a machine, from our bodies and their place in the natural world.

The *mitwelt*, or 'with-world', concerns the social world and our relationships with other human beings. Whilst the fundamentally social nature of human beings is well-recognised within existentialist philosophy, this does not mean that we should treat it simply as the background to our lives. The mitwelt concerns our relationship with our world and what this means to us. Obviously relationships with others will form a central part of this dimension, but this may include relationships with people from our past, imaginary work on possible future relationships, alongside dealing with relationships in the present. Identifying patterns of relating are key here as clients tell us through dialogue and also directly through the relationship to the therapist much about the social aspects of their world, which so often forms the basis for problems in living. Perhaps the best articulation/development of this dimension comes through the work of Buber (1923/1958) and his notion of I–Thou relating, which is discussed in detail in Chapter 8.

The *eigenwelt*, or 'own-world' (sometimes called the psychological world) concerns our sense of self. At birth we emerge into a world in which we are in relation with others with no sense of self (see Langdridge, 2005a, for a discussion of this drawing on Merleau-Ponty). It is only later as we develop and become able to reflect on ourselves that a nascent sense of self appears. Through adolescence we begin to firm up our understanding of who we are, creating a sense of an inner world, and our place in the world in relation to others, culminating in what is popularly (though inaccurately) called our 'personality'. How we understand ourselves is crucial for our engagement in the world, and forms the basis for much psychotherapeutic work. Some severe human conditions, invariably classified as schizoid or personality disorders within the psychiatric professions, appear to involve a failure to develop or engage with the eigenwelt, with instead a relationship with the world that is almost entirely physical or social. However, even in more everyday functioning there may be times when the eigenwelt is apparently lost and the person becomes predominantly caught up in the physical or social. Furthermore, distortions occurring at the level of the eigenwelt may well be revealed when working with people experiencing depressive conditions. Here we often see that nothing in the social world can seemingly penetrate or be held within the eigenwelt of the client and sustained such that the mood may shift or be transformed.

The final dimension is a later addition, seemingly overlooked by Binswanger, and concerns spiritual aspects of life. The *überwelt* (or 'above-world') is a fourth dimension first articulated by Emmy van Deurzen in 1984 (then Deurzen-Smith, 1984, 1988). She proposed this addition to the three dimensions of Binswanger to bring to the fore a concern within the lifeworld for spiritual matters or the meaning of life. This dimension should not be confused with having a religious belief (though of course this may provide a sense of meaning of life for some people) but concerns a person's system of meaning and values for living, and so cuts across the physical, psychological and social dimensions. We are all born into and brought up in a particular ideological setting and this is very likely to influence the way we see the world. We may accept or reject those foundational values as we develop and encounter alternative belief systems, but ultimately we can never escape ideology. We inevitably inhabit a belief system which will guide our actions in the world, although there may be times when we become out of touch with our beliefs or find them in opposition to other aspects of how we are living and this is where a therapeutic focus on the spiritual may well prove useful. The late-modern times that we are living through in the West often seem to be devoid of any sense of spirituality, but this is not a necessary truth. Seemingly superficial values (such as the desire for fame or celebrity, the pursuit of wealth at all costs) belong to an ideological system, one which appears dominant today. However, we can decide for ourselves whether this is a belief system that we want to embrace or reject. People can become caught up in belief systems that are at odds with other aspects of their life and feel deeply dissatisfied with the world, and it is here that they might find greater reward in re-thinking the values that underpin their existence. Change at the level of the überwelt can often prove to lead to some of the most profound change in living for us all.

Activity Produce a written inventory of your own life mapped against the four dimensions outlined above. This could be presented as a table with the four dimensions across the top and your evaluation of how well you engage in each dimension in rows below. Do you engage in the world predominantly in one or two dimensions or evenly across all four (which is probably not likely for most of us)? Do you feel that you neglect any dimensions in your life? If so, what might you do to address this lack? Remember it does not mean you have serious problems if from time to time you focus on particular dimensions (it may simply be a reflection of current issues in your life), though it is often a useful process to check yourself (as a trainee or practising therapist) every now and again.

So what does this all mean for practice? In many ways these ideas are some of the simplest yet most useful existential concepts to supplement the phenomenological method. They can be used as a useful guide to the material being presented by a client, watching out for their movement within and between the four realms of experience. A client may talk about their life referring to only a limited number of the four dimensions or may omit one altogether (no talk about the meaning of life or spirituality, for instance). There may be a central concern with only one dimension (their physical appearance) and little consideration of other aspects of their lifeworld. What we do with this information requires careful thought on a case-by-case basis. It may be useful, for instance, to bring up issues in a neglected dimension with a client and assess their response. Or indeed it might even be useful to mention to a client that they only seem to be concerned with one aspect of their experience and then explore the possible impact of this on any problems they are facing. Whilst we generally follow our clients when working as existential therapists, this does not mean we are passive in the relationship. There will be times with many clients when we might wish to intervene in proceedings and reflect on what is being spoken about, or intervene more directly and raise new topics for discussion. A client may not wish to explore a new topic and we cannot and should not force them to do so, but more often than not such an intervention allows for an opening-up in the work that is productive.

Case study   Naomi and her immersion in the everyday

Naomi is a bright 30-year-old woman, working very successfully in industry after previously gaining a first-class degree in psychology from Oxford sponsored by her present employers. She works very long hours and is also involved in a charity she co-founded, which takes up much of her free time. She enjoys a healthy sex life when she has the time and previously had a relationship of seven years with a man she met at university, which she ended: 'it had been on and off for the last few years anyway'. She came to see me as she could not understand why she so readily felt gloomy about life. In her own words she 'had nothing to worry about and so much going on' but still she would find herself feeling melancholy without any known cause. Naomi was in many ways a classic client for existential therapy as there did not appear to be anything profoundly wrong with her life yet still she felt a lack of passion for life. She lost her father during her teenage years, which marked a radical break in how she saw the world. Prior to his death there had been considerable certainty and a sense of security in the world, but following this she was not sure of the permanence or purpose of anything anymore. We explored the impact of her father's early death and how she had responded, and she understood what impact this event had on her but claimed this had little impact on her now. I decided to shift focus to the present and explore the various aspects of her life through the lens of the four dimensions.

It became apparent that Naomi was consumed with the everyday, albeit in a highly disguised form. Whilst the founding of a charity may appear to relate to a desire to make the world a better place (and so speak to spiritual aspects of existence) this was not primarily the case for Naomi, but instead simply another way to lose herself in work, to exist only for others in the social world. This emerged as a subtle pattern of behaviour, with a clear gap in Naomi's lifeworld as it related to the meaning of life. Life had no meaning since the death of her father and she avoided having to face up to this by immersing herself in the everyday of others (through excessive work or hedonism). Our work focussed on how Naomi might first give herself space to feel the impact of her early loss on her present existence and use these feelings to identify what she cared about now. She did in fact care about the charity she founded, even though this had been disavowed and lost in her all consuming work ethic, and she began to realise that she could do something meaningful. However, this was still not enough to shift her low mood and we moved on to examining her relationships, which whilst apparently rich and satisfying on the surface did not actually involve her feeling truly connected with others. Her previous relationship with her boyfriend had given her glimpses into the power of the social world for her and this had scared her, resulting in her avoiding a real commitment. She recognised this and that if she were to move forward she might need to stay with the complex feelings evoked by intimate relationships and explore whether these enriched her in a way that was not readily apparent.

Working with dreams

Working with dreams was a mainstay of classical psychoanalysis, though is considered less crucial amongst many contemporary psychotherapists today. For many in both psychoanalytic and existential therapies, however, dreams do still offer up considerable potential for working with clients to illuminate aspects of their experience. It provides a meta-dimension that stands over and above the four dimensions discussed above where we can work together with our clients to critically examine their lifeworld. The earliest existential work on dream analysis was conducted by Binswanger (1958) and Boss (1957), both of whom sought to shift psychotherapeutic dream analysis away from its psychoanalytic roots. For Freud (1900) dreams served to preserve sleep, providing a means for working through unresolved anxiety through representations of wishes that would otherwise be unacceptable to the dreamer. That is, dreams invariably involved some latent (or hidden) meaning that disguised their true meaning and needed to be subject to an analysis. Contemporary psychoanalysts have increasingly shifted to focus on working with the dreamer to understand the nature of the dream itself. This move echoes the transformation initiated by Boss, in particular, who sought to shift from a focus on the latent to a focus on the manifest content of the dream. Boss (ibid.) draws extensively on Heidegger (1927/1962) to produce an alternative to psychoanalytic dream analysis. He argues that an analysis of dreams must be treated similarly to an analysis of material produced in the waking world. The dream world, whilst superficially different from the waking world, reveals a person's current concerns, much as material does in the waking world. Dream analysis, on this basis, becomes a phenomenological exercise in which the therapist and client work together to elucidate the manifest meaning of any dream presented. That is, the analysis of dreams appears to be akin to the analysis of all other material presented by the client, with the potential to offer further insights into a person's way of engaging (or not) with their world. Cohn (1997: 84) describes the existential approach to dream analysis as follows:

> The phenomenologist instead of distinguishing between surface and depth, tries to establish ever-widening contexts. Thus there cannot be a distinction between 'manifest' and 'latent' dream contents. But Boss rightly stresses that existential psychotherapy 'agrees with psychoanalytic experience that those realms of the human world which find admittance into the light of the dreaming Dasein are those a human being has not become aware of in his waking state' (Boss, 1963: 262). However, as Boss also emphasises, dreams are not something we 'have', they are an aspect of our being – 'we are our dreaming state' (1963: 261). They are not puzzles to be solved but openings to be attended to.

Jaenicke (1996), following Boss, argues that dreams show what matters to us, ontologically speaking, in the most important way: 'dreams, just like moods, confront us with our being-in-the-world as it matters to us' (p. 107). Jaenicke further explains that 'dreams embody and point to the ontological inclusion of our current ontic concerns' (ibid.). This is important, for it suggests that an analysis of dreams may give us privileged access not only to a person's ontic (or everyday) concerns but also insights into their ontological foundation. Dreams should therefore occupy a central part of existential therapy. There has been relatively little more work than this, however, in developing an existential approach to dream analysis, at least in the English language literature. The exception to this is my own attempt to further elaborate an existential approach to dream analysis (Langdridge, 2006), which I discuss below.

In my 2006 paper on dream analysis I propose a number of additions to the method of dream analysis first proposed by Boss, notably the use of 'fractions of the lifeworld' (Ashworth, 2003a, 2003b), alongside the concept of narrative identity (Ricoeur, 1988, 1992), to interrogate the manifest content of a dream. For me, dreams offer a unique opportunity to work with a client on a discrete piece of material. They are invariably presented differently from the everyday stuff of psychotherapy, neatly packaged and presented to the therapist and, as such, are amenable to the analytic tools more frequently seen in phenomenological research methods. Ashworth (ibid.) has elaborated a method of phenomenological analysis that incorporates what he terms 'fractions of the lifeworld', which might also be referred to as *existentials* or the givens of existence. These include:

- Selfhood (or identity, which I further elaborated as 'narrative identity')
- Sociality (or relationality/intersubjectivity)
- Embodiment
- Temporality
- Spatiality
- Project (this is a concept from Sartre that will be discussed in the next chapter)
- Discourse (or the way in which language shapes the world)

And I would add:

- Being-towards-death

When conducting an analysis of research data one would draw on these existentials to interrogate the data collected (via an interview, for instance). One or more of these elements is likely to be relevant and by using these ideas it becomes possible to gain greater insight into the phenomenon that is being investigated. My own suggestion within existential dream analysis is to employ a similar method working with the client to analyse their dream material together. This requires several passes through the dream story, each time drawing on a different existential to further elucidate the content of the story being recounted. For this to work, the first step is to encourage clients to keep a dream diary. Few people remember their dreams in much detail unless encouraged to do this. The best method is for people to use a diary and get into the routine of writing down their dreams immediately upon waking. Should there be any delay in actively remembering a dream then it is likely to dissipate from conscious thought. By writing down dreams upon waking this likelihood is greatly reduced. Clients are then invited to present dreams within therapy as they see fit. It is not necessary to continually interrogate dreams recounted in a diary, but instead the client has control through their own choosing of what they wish to present at what time within the therapeutic process. When a client presents a dream the normal therapeutic process is temporarily suspended as the dream becomes the focus of analysis. It is useful to encourage the client to recount the dream in the first person, as if they were dreaming it in the moment of presentation. On the first pass it is simply a case of listening with a phenomenological attitude to the content, asking questions of clarification. However, upon further readings the therapist is able to draw on the fractions listed above to explore different elements of the dream, repeating this process using different fractions until all possible meaning is exhausted. Through this method greater insight is gained into the existential content of the dream, with the possibility of illuminating the lifeworld of the dreamer and their ontological concerns in greater detail.

Case study Daljeet and his escape by bus

Daljeet recounted a dream. He was in a house, unknown to him but with French doors which were swinging open. He was with his partner arguing about her plans to go out and meet a male friend 'as it was their birthday' that evening. Daljeet did not know who this friend was or how his partner Karen knew him. He was hoping to hear more about them and some explanation for this arrangement to meet someone he had never heard of before. Karen was indifferent to Daljeet's concerns and simply said he was a friend. When Daljeet pressed further about where they were meeting Karen replied 'I don't know, I'll find out when I get there' and continued to get ready to leave. Daljeet was infuriated and also deeply troubled about this. He never got to meet Karen's friends and felt torn between giving her space to be with her friends alone and being excluded from being a part of her life. They had been together for two years and yet there was a secretive quality that disturbed Daljeet. He left and jumped on the first bus he saw, with his partner shouting after him. He planned to get off just round the corner and return to deal with things but the bus never stopped, just continued to drive on and on until he was finally able to get off the bus. He had no idea where he was and then awoke with a start. He remained troubled by this dream when waking as he felt it reflected some of the issues about his relationship with Karen that were currently worrying him.

In working with Daljeet on this dream we sought to draw out the detail of the dream, which when first presented was simply highlights, with me encouraging Daljeet to retell the dream in the first person as I asked about detail. This was a simple exercise in phenomenology as I sought to encourage him to elaborate the detail of the dream in a coherent manner. This process proved valuable as Daljeet had not mentioned the detail concerning his escape on a bus in the first account given. I then suggested we work through the dream a number of times examining it for different qualities each time (the fractions of the lifeworld). The first pass through concerned mood and the emotional quality of different moments. Through this we discovered how torn Daljeet felt about the dimension of freedom versus possessiveness. He wanted to allow freedom in his relationship with his partner but had strong possessive feelings towards her. When we explored this he realised that these were being driven by a sense that he felt she was not trustworthy and might act irresponsibly, especially when drinking alcohol. He had some evidence to support this and so felt this was not necessarily an inappropriate way to feel in spite of it causing him difficulties. Spatiality also proved to be an important factor in the dream when we examined it. There was an inherent tension expressed as we analysed the dream between a sense of closeness between Daljeet and Karen and distance when trouble emerged, exemplified by the desire for him to escape (in this case by bus). I asked about the bus journey and how it did not stop as expected with him finding himself somewhere unfamiliar. This was an important aspect of the dream, as Daljeet realised that running away would result in more uncertainty than staying with his partner, in spite of their difficulties. There was a realisation of what might be lost that was often masked in his waking world through argument and animosity. The final fraction that proved important concerned his sense of selfhood and how his eigenwelt had become enmeshed with the mitwelt. His world of relating had both opened up – as experienced with Karen – and closed down with others. He spent most of his time with Karen and neglected other relationships, with a sense of jealousy and abandonment emerging when Karen met with her friends. There was a one-sidedness to this though as Daljeet felt Karen encouraged their inter-dependence when it suited her but abandoned it when she wanted to escape with others. What was revealed was how this dream gave us insight into many pressing concerns that were troubling Daljeet in his waking world and how he was responding to them. The detailed analysis we engaged in opened up new avenues for discussion in our work together that proved productive in enabling Daljeet to better understand himself and his relations with others.

Further reading

Boss, M. (1957). *The analysis of dreams* (trans. A. J. Pomerans). London: Rider.
    A full and comprehensive account of the existential method of dream analysis, drawing on Heidegger, proposed by Medard Boss.

Langdridge, D. (2006). Imaginative variations on selfhood: elaborating an existential-phenomenological approach to dream analysis. *Existential Analysis, 17*(1) 2–13.
    A detailed statement of my own extension of the approach to dream analysis of Boss, drawing further on aspects of phenomenological methodology.

May, R., Angel, E. & Ellenberger, H.F. (1958). *Existence*. New York: Basic Books.
    An early statement of the fundamentals of existential analysis. The book includes chapters by Rollo May and Ludwig Binswanger with comprehensive coverage of the three dimensions of existence and a number of lengthy case studies.

SEVEN Freedom, Choice and Responsibility

CHAPTER AIMS

This chapter aims to:

- provide an introduction to a number of key ideas central to existential therapeutic practice including: freedom, choice and project, and bad faith;
- explain how these philosophical concepts can be applied in practice;
- provide a number of case studies to show the value of these different concepts in different therapeutic situations.

Freedom, choice and project

Freedom and choice are concepts that form the mainstay of all existential philosophy, being stressed in Kierkegaard, Nietzsche and Heidegger. It is, however, in the work of Jean Paul Sartre (1905–1980) that we see these concepts realised most powerfully, though not without some problems. Sartre is the philosopher whose work is most clearly identified with existentialism and arguably represents the zenith of existential philosophy. For Sartre (1943/1956) the heart of existentialism is that existence precedes essence. That is, human beings do not have any essential self or personality that makes us what we are. We create ourselves (our existence) and through this process only later come to recognise any essence to our understanding of selfhood. This runs counter to much previous philosophy (such as the work of Plato and Descartes) and also much contemporary theory in counselling, psychotherapy and psychology. A crucial distinction here is between two modes of consciousness: the *pre-reflective* and the *reflective*. The pre-reflective is the primary mode of consciousness, in which there is no awareness of self. The reflective mode, on the other hand, refers to our awareness of selfhood, through memory for instance. The pre-reflective concerns our intentional relationship to the world and is, therefore, the primary mode of being but which is always accessible to reflective consciousness as we are always necessarily 'aware of being aware'. The result of this distinction with an empty reflective consciousness is freedom. The lack of any essence results in an unavoidable freedom at the heart of human being with us not just the sum of the facts of our existence but able to make of our lives what we will.

A further important distinction for Sartre (1943/1956) is between *facticity* and *transcendence*, with our facticity concerning our biology, history, the society to which we belong, and transcendence our freedom, our capacity to negate (or transcend) those given facts about our existence. Facticity therefore concerns those givens about our existence which we cannot change. In Heidegger's terms, we are thrown into a world and the time and place of our birth result in certain facts about our life that we cannot change, whether this refers to our body, our family or our culture. The key thing for Sartre, however, is what we make of our facticity, and he argues that we can make of it what we will. Human existence is ultimately a process in which we negate or transcend the facts of our existence, making choices about what we do and who we are to become and interpreting the brute facts of existence in different ways. Whilst a person born blind can never change that fact of their existence, they can decide what this means and how they will live their life accordingly in the face of this element of their facticity.

A further important distinction for Sartre is between being-for-itself (*être-pour-soi*) and being-in-itself (*être-en-soi*). These terms relate to the notions of facticity and transcendence but are not synonymous with them or the reflective and pre-reflective, discussed above. Being-for-itself refers to those creatures with the capacity for self-reflection, though this is not restricted solely to reflective consciousness (and so incorporates both the reflective and pre-reflective elements of consciousness: that is, all consciousness). Freedom is at the heart of being-for-itself, with the capacity to negate (or transcend) the in-itself, to become what it is not. Being-in-itself, by contrast, is all that which is not consciousness, that which is given. Sartre is clear that we cannot speak directly of the in-itself as it is in itself, as any attempt to do so ascribes it meaning (via the for-itself). There is no possibility of a neutral encounter with the in-itself and instead it is through our facticity, which we can reflect upon, that we see the relationship between being-for-itself and being-in-itself. This distinction is, for Sartre, a phenomenological description of the nature of being and one which enables us to appreciate how human existence involves 'no-thingness', no essential structure but instead freedom, a process of negation/transcendence beyond what is given. The distinction between the in-itself and for-itself may, at first, appear dualist and some commentators have criticised Sartre for this, but the distinction is not simply between two different kinds of stuff (with all the problems that follow from this) as we see with Descartes but between two different modes of being, the being that is exclusive to human existence and the being of 'mere objects'. There is clearly a dualism at work here, even if this is somewhat different from the dualism of Descartes, and Sartre himself acknowledged this distinction as problematic/artificial in *Being and Nothingness* itself, noting that these are not terms that can exist in isolation.

Out of this distinction Sartre evinces a tripartite argument for freedom (Reynolds, 2006). This argument revolves around the notion of *negation*, which Sartre (unlike Heidegger) directly links with nothingness. Sartre (ibid.)

goes into considerable detail developing his argument, which need not concern us here, though the interested reader will find a very clear explanation in Reynolds (ibid.). The most illuminating element in his argument emerges when Sartre (ibid.), in typical style, provides an example of an everyday situation to evidence his assertion about freedom through negation. He describes the situation of a person going into a café, expecting to meet a friend, who sees immediately that they are not there. The café and all other people become background against which they expect their friend to stand out, and with this negation emerges in our perception of the world. The café and other people disappear from our awareness, in an act of negation, and the absence of our friend further represents a *perceived* absence, an actual experience of negation or nothingness (no-thing-ness or non-being).

An important consequence of this freedom is the *anguish* that results from the nothingness ('no-thing-ness') at the heart of human existence. Anguish is the state that results from our awareness of our own freedom. This is distinct from fear, which involves a response to some threat in the world, as anguish results from our awareness of our sense of self and the freedom we have to respond to a situation in any number of different ways. Nothingness evokes anguish because it is a part of us and we cannot escape it or immerse ourselves completely in any other project. We can never achieve the solidity and certainty of an object like a tree but must instead live with the anguish of knowing we are 'no-thing', needing to make choices about who or what we are to become.

Activity   Think of a time when you were faced with a choice. Write about that moment in the present tense as if you were back there again. Tune in to your feelings and try to elaborate these as you write. What came up for you? Did the sense of freedom promote anguish? Perhaps you felt this differently or would use different terms to describe the sense of needing to decide something for yourself.

Freedom, in these existential terms, may be contrasted with causal explanatory frameworks for human behaviour (psychoanalysis and evolutionary psychology being good examples). In causal models there is a belief that present behaviour can be explained by prior causes, whether these be early childhood trauma or our ancient hunter-gatherer past. Sartre's example of two hikers brings this distinction to life. He describes the situation of two hikers walking a long distance with fatigue setting in and both struggling against this to continue to walk. One of them gives up whilst the other continues to press on. Assuming both are similar physically, what is it that leads one to give up whilst the other fights harder against their fatigue to press on? Advocates of causal models of human behaviour might simply account for this on the basis of a weakness of personality: one is less tenacious than the other. For Sartre, and all other existentialists, this is not a causal explanation in the way that we know that influenza explains a high temperature, but rather a way of simply describing patterns of behaviour being observed. Nothing determines the decision to give up. We retain responsibility for our actions even when under duress or facing extreme conditions. This position presents a problem, however, which is to reconcile freedom with responsibility. Sartre seeks to achieve this through the notion of a *fundamental project*, or original choice. The notion of a fundamental project is, in essence, the unity of the for-itself, the motivation which drives us through life. The fundamental project concerns our stance towards life, whether it be to always engage tenaciously or to give in to a struggle, and for Sartre is something freely chosen early in life. For the hiker who decided to stop when encountering fatigue there was a sense in which continuing was at odds with their fundamental project, with their stance towards the world. Perhaps such a physical overcoming was not important, with them focusing elsewhere on gaining a sense of achievement. The key thing is that all decisions relate to the meaning any one person gives a situation, which is itself part of the totality of who that person is but not simply the result of prior causes. This is a subtle distinction and it is all too easy to reduce the notion of project to a causal personality theory, which would be a grave error. Instead, it should be seen as the means by which we can understand our everyday ways of engaging in the world, our own understanding of what matters and what drives us through life. Sartre believes that an existential psychoanalysis must concern itself with a hermeneutic analysis of lived experience in order to reveal the fundamental project of any particular for-itself. Sartre (1952/1964, 1971) engaged in such analyses (though not within a therapeutic setting) on a number of important public figures, including Jean Genet, Baudelaire and Flaubert, and whilst these analyses are often insightful and revealing they are not without their problems. The notion of a fundamental project, or originary choice, is deeply problematic and something strongly criticised by Maurice Merleau-Ponty (1908–1961), a philosophical contemporary of Sartre (more below). However, for many clients in therapy there is certainly often a poorly conceived sense of project, or one which is at odds with how they want to live, and this may form the basis of productive discussion.

A Sartrean account of freedom and choice appears at times to ignore the influence of the social world and, in particular, inequality and de Beauvoir (1947/1976), whose work is intimately related to that of Sartre, provides a more socially grounded expression of freedom whilst building on the same principles. In many ways Sartre's views were a reflection of his justifiable concerns, living through the Second World War, about the abrogation of responsibility demonstrated by individuals complicit in the oppression of others. But is it true that we all have the capacity to make of a situation what we will, even accepting that this is subject to our fundamental project, or are some in a more privileged position than others to realise themselves?

De Beauvoir (1949/1972) in *The Second Sex*, her feminist anthropological treatise on the problem of woman as *Other*, develops the notion of bad faith, providing a more subtle and less global understanding of how people, though women in particular, might deal with the anguish of freedom. She proposes three main ways in which women might be complicit in their subjugation and therefore act in bad faith (from Reynolds, 2006):

- **Narcissist:** a focus on, and valuing of, herself as a beautiful object for the other.
- **Woman in love:** exclusive investment, through a relationship, in a privileged male object.
- **Mystic:** exclusive investment in the absolute or God.

Here we see themes that still resonate today even with the impact of feminism, with women feeling the need to engage in such acts of bad faith within a male-dominated world. It is in her principal philosophical text, *The Ethics of Ambiguity*, however, that de Beauvoir (1947/1976) really challenges the (arguably over-simplistic) notion of freedom in Sartre's philosophy. She argues that women who have been subject to sustained oppression (and I would want to extend this to any other categories of oppressed persons) may be unable to see other possibilities beyond their current situation and may, therefore, be unable to conceive of anything other than bad faith. This point is reflected in social movements (such as the feminist, lesbian, gay, bi, trans, anti-capitalist and so on) which inevitably need to engage in a process of consciousness-raising amongst their members in order that people come to realise that there might be an alternative to their current position in the world.

De Beauvoir (ibid.) provides a much more grounded and politically astute understanding of freedom and choice than Sartre, recognising that oppression works against some groups (such as women) more than others. She recognises the way that freedom is always counterposed against the social world in which choices are made in practice, resulting in an ambiguous mix of transcendence and facticity. To this end, and in contrast to Sartre (see below), she argues that a person's transcendence and freedom requires the freedom and transcendence of others. Oppressed groups in particular need to work with others sharing a common goal to challenge oppression and find new ways of living. De Beauvoir does not abandon Sartre's insistence that all human beings transcend their facticity but develops this in recognising that amongst those who are oppressed the gap between their facticity and goals may be so great that they are condemned to failure. That is, reciprocal transcendence is only possible when there is social equality.

> The trick of tyrants is to enclose man (*sic*) in the immanence of his facticity and to try to forget that he is always, as Heidegger puts it 'infinitely more than he would be if he were reduced to being what he is' … man is a being of the distances, a movement toward the future, a project. (De Beauvoir, 1947/1976: 102)

The particular positive emphasis on choice that Sartre espouses has also been criticised by Merleau-Ponty (1945/1962), who goes much further than de Beauvoir, for the way in which he believes Sartre fails to account for the socially and historically embedded nature of existence. Merleau-Ponty argues that Sartre over-states the positive case for freedom, missing a number of key elements in his understanding. First, there is the problem that Sartre believes any choice stands alone and can therefore be inverted or overturned and transform a person's situation in the world. Whilst this might be true of some choices it is, for Merleau-Ponty, certainly not the case for all, if we are to use choice in any meaningful sense. A person who was formerly a Christian may choose to become a Muslim, but any real sense of transformation such that the world appears as it would to a Muslim cannot happen 'just like that'. It takes time and immersion in a new set of beliefs or culture to truly understand what it is like to see the world from a fundamentally different perspective. This is not a simple case of needing the will to believe differently, but rather reflective of the need for a proper understanding before it becomes possible to have the will to believe. This position reasserts Heidegger's recognition of the *thrownness* of existence and how we enter the world in a particular place, time and, therefore, culture, providing limits to our understanding. Ironically, given Sartre's criticisms of Husserl, he himself appears to have lost sight of the situated nature of existence and offers up a naïve sense of freedom detached from the practical and material reality of life.

Merleau-Ponty's criticism also has profound implications for Sartre's notion of a fundamental project. If the fundamental project, or original choice, involves understanding (which surely it must), how can this emerge out of nothing? If our project shapes our stance towards the world and motivates our actions within it, then how can an initial choice be made? Furthermore, any suggestion that such a choice could be made early in life, in childhood for instance, makes little sense as we need the experience of life to even begin to be able to make choices about how we want to live. This does not result in a loss of freedom within existentialism, however. Merleau-Ponty argues that Sartre is confused when he ties freedom and choice together, as a positive choice is not a requirement for freedom. Much of life is lived with us engaging pre-reflectively in the lived world with only occasional moments of choice, in the Sartrean sense. At all times we have the power to refuse, the power to decide not to do something rather than be carried along with it, but this is quite a different situation to seeing us all continuously engaged in reflective processes of choice about who we are and what we are doing. So, instead of initial choice and an overly positive conception of choice (inextricably tied to freedom) we see, with Merleau-Ponty, the importance of the *power to refuse*, our fundamental freedom to exert our will and act when needed.

Case study   Marion and the anguish of freedom

Marion is in her early thirties, bisexual and beginning to explore the possibility of polyamorous relationships (multiple open loving relationships). She presented for a number of seemingly disparate reasons: her concern about a lack of experience with relationships (always feeling she was lagging behind everyone else); a feeling that she had lost direction in her work; and a sense of not having carved out a secure sense of home. We spent the first few months exploring these different issues, which with clarification all appeared linked. Marion described a sense of being developmentally delayed and always feeling the need to catch up with others. Her thoughts about relationships were particularly pertinent with her believing that a form of ethical non-monogamy made sense to her. Whilst I strongly support such relationship choices and see many clients happily engaged in such arrangements, I began to feel that this might not be the best choice for Marion. All her talk of what she wanted as she lurched from perceived crisis to crisis spoke to a sense of uncertainty about her choice for ethical non-monogamy. Whenever I challenged her on this she would always muster up an intellectual defence, which was then backed up by speaking to her ability to sustain the ambiguity and complexity that may follow from adopting an unconventional lifestyle. After several months Marion appeared to be in crisis, with her feeling unable to cope with all that life was throwing at her. She spoke of her problems managing the relationships she was engaged with and her deep distress around them. She also spoke of her stress at work and general sense of having no foundation in life. It was clear to Marion and myself that given she could not sustain herself in her present situation she needed to make a choice: to leave a relationship, to change job, to move home, something, anything, that might free up space for her to lay some firm foundations. With discussion of every potential choice, Marion simply could not contemplate it ('There is too much going on for me at the moment to make any drastic choices') and became increasingly distressed. She knew she could choose, but the more she realised this the more she experienced the anguish that follows from such freedom. The paradoxical nature of her inability to effect change in spite of her distress at her current situation appeared to escape her. With time Marion's situation changed as she felt more comfortable with one of her relationships, and with this she became more able to face the anguish of her freedom and realise that she needed to effect change in her world. This led to her ending the other relationship and moving home. These were not easy decisions and she remained uncertain whether these might be closing down possibilities, but the ongoing distress she felt (alongside a sense of some certainty with the other relationship) enabled her to face the anguish of her freedom more readily than before. In time Marion came to realise that whilst ethical non-monogamy made sense to her intellectually, the version she attempted did not meet her needs, as felt, and she began to slowly revise her views on this aspect of her identity and focus instead on a less open (though still polyamorous) form of relating.

Self-deception (*mauvais foi*)

A key element in Sartre's arguments about freedom is the notion of *bad faith* (*mauvais foi* in French). Indeed, bad faith operates as the starting point for freedom, for it is through his demonstration of the possibility of bad faith that he realises the nothingness of human consciousness. But what is bad faith exactly? In many ways bad faith is the Sartrean equivalent of Heidegger's inauthenticity. As Beings-for-themselves have, at the very least, a pre-reflective awareness of themselves, they are conscious of the fact that they are not like other things, and upon realising that they are subject to boundless freedom they suffer anguish. In order to alleviate this anguish all Beings-for-themselves – all of us – must employ bad faith. Bad faith is an example of a *project* in which the freedom of the for-itself is discarded and instead one adopts the position of the in-itself. All projects stem from an original *fundamental project,* realised early in life when the for-itself becomes aware of his or her freedom.

Sartre once again provides some vivid, though not unproblematic, examples to illustrate this concept. The most well-known example of bad faith is also arguably the most problematic. Sartre describes the situation as follows. A woman is with a man in a café. It is potentially the start of a relationship, but given it is so early on the woman is uncertain how to proceed. During conversation the man grasps the woman's hand. The woman, being uncertain about things, neither wants to return his advance by acknowledging his grasp nor rebuff him by removing his hand, and so instead she leaves her hand there pretending to herself that it has not happened. She is, of course, making a choice (in spite of her reluctance to choose: between acceptance or rejection), but here it is a choice not to choose. She divorces her thinking from her body and pretends nothing has happened in spite of wanting to accept his advance, and with this she is in bad faith.

This account has been the subject of some criticism, particularly by feminist writers, for the way in which it represents a bigger problem in Sartre's writing about the place of women in his thought (Reynolds, 2006). Le Doeuff (1991) first questions how Sartre, a man, can possibly know what is going on in the mind of this woman, and second, argues that Sartre fails to account for the prevailing socio-cultural conditions of the time in which he was writing. The situation for women in the 1940s in France was quite different from today, and whilst today it may be commonplace for a woman to confidently express her own needs and desires (though even this is not so free of patriarchal demands), this was certainly not the case in the 1940s. In many ways, de Beauvoir's work represents a healthy corrective to this tendency in Sartre, providing a more socio-culturally grounded foundation to his philosophy, and when the two philosophies are combined they are both, in my view, much more powerfully realised.

How might bad faith be relevant to therapy? Well, it is similar to the notion of authenticity and given that both are thought to occur all the time is certainly likely to show itself in the consulting room. Many clients struggle to recognise the choices that they have available, noting the need to recognise the practical limits that are placed on freedom, and as such exist in bad faith, as we all do from time to time. In the case study below I highlight one example, but there are many more which are much more commonplace when we see clients struggling to take action to change their situation in spite of it feeling wrong for them. This can be anything from decisions about work and careers to relationships. Bad faith needs to be handled sensitively, however. A crude intervention on the part of the therapist suggesting that a client can easily change is never likely to be helpful. Sartre's views need to be tempered by those of de Beauvoir and Merleau-Ponty, with appropriate recognition of the way in which freedom, whilst fundamental to human existence, is also situated and limited by the social world into which we are thrown. The focus must always be on the client coming to realise what is possible for themselves, with gentle encouragement and challenge from the therapist. If we leap in for them they will likely not have the space to effect change and face the anguish of existence head-on with the necessary courage required.

Case study   Sam and his flight from freedom

Sam is in his late forties, single and still living at home with his parents. He came to see me having been referred by another therapist to discuss his thoughts and feelings about his sexuality. Meeting Sam was a curious experience as I quickly realised that he lacked any sense of being psychologically minded. He operated in a factual way and did not have much capacity for reflection. Rather than abandon him I adjusted my way of working to meet him, offering much more practical advice and engagement than I would ordinarily. With this we were able to find a way of relating which worked. He discussed his sexual fantasies, which were what many would consider the normal stuff of a gay man, but he wrapped these up in a rather old-fashioned notion of questioning his sex (whether he might really be a woman). Upon exploring this, he had no real belief that he was a woman but rather that this was the only way in which he could think of wanting to be penetrated by a man. We discussed what a gay identity might mean and it emerged that he had long had these feelings and yet continually resisted identifying with them. In a sense he was in bad faith, detaching himself from his sexual feelings much like the woman in the café detaches herself from her hand. Whilst this concept providing some purchase for understanding this situation, the failure of Sartre to account for the social context (much like his failure to account for the socio-cultural conditions for women when describing the example above) for me meant that this concept, had it been employed ruthlessly, would have been destructive. Instead, I worked with Sam to recognise the social world into which he was thrown, the homonegativity and heterosexism he had to grow up with, whilst also recognising that he did have the power to refuse heterosexuality (to move out of bad faith) and integrate his sexual feelings with his sense of selfhood. Much of this work involved me coaching Sam through small steps to take action, and then us working to explore what this was like for him. He came out to his parents and his friends and also moved out of home for the first time in his life. He remained uneasy with his feelings and struggled with sexual acts themselves at first, but he made considerable progress and demonstrated enormous courage in the process. I continued to see Sam on an occasional basis for the next two years and during this time witnessed him taking charge of his life at his own pace, seeking me out for conversation and support in the decisions he was making when he felt he needed it. He has clearly found a way of embracing life, living more authentically and realising his possibilities much more fully.

Further reading

De Beauvoir, S. (1947/1976). *The ethics of ambiguity* (trans. B. Frechtman). New York: Kensington.
De Beauvoir, S. (1949/1972). *The second sex* (trans. H. Parshley). Harmondsworth: Penguin.
   Two classic texts by de Beauvoir, both of which are remarkably accessible.

Sartre, J.-P. (1943/1956). *Being and nothingness: an essay on phenomenological ontology* (trans. H. Barnes). New York: Philosophical Library.
   Another classic that is not easy going but another 'must read' for the aspiring existential therapist.

EIGHT   Relatedness

CHAPTER AIMS

This chapter aims to:

- provide an introduction to one key idea central to existential therapeutic practice, that of relatedness;
- explain how different understandings of this philosophical concept can be applied in practice;
- provide a number of case studies to show the value of relatedness within different therapeutic situations.

Kierkegaard and Nietzsche both emphasise a sense of individuality in their philosophy and calls for *inwardness*. Kierkegaard does, of course, speak of the need for concern for others and commitment to the social world in his religious stage, but it is really with Heidegger within the existential tradition that we see an emphasis on relatedness. Heidegger's concern is ontological and so whilst the notion of *Being-with* (or *Mitsein*) captures something fundamental about existence, it does not provide us with much more than a starting point for practice (see Chapter 3). Indeed, it was confusion about the ontological and the ontic that led Binswanger (1958, 1963) to elaborate his own theory of love (as an essential element of the social world: *mitwelt*), as he thought this was missing in Heidegger's work. Consideration of the mitwelt is a crucial element in pretty much all psychotherapy, and the focus in this chapter is on those writers who have articulated an understanding of relatedness in much more detail and which is of direct relevance to the practice of existential therapy.

The therapeutic relationship

First of all, why is the relationship so central in all counselling and psychotherapy? Well, the research literature is quite clear that a good therapeutic relationship is a key factor for successful client outcomes and also the client's perception of the value of the experience (see Cooper, 2008, for a review). Lambert (Asay and Lambert, 1999) found that approximately 30 per cent of effective therapeutic outcomes can be attributed to relational factors (with others – e.g. Krupnik et al., 1996 – finding a lower but still significant percentage). Self-report findings from clients also indicate the quality of the relationship to be the most important factor in their experience (Bohart and Tallman, 1999). There is little doubt now that a good therapeutic relationship is not only crucial for the process of therapy itself but is also in itself a significant factor in successful outcomes for clients.

The work of Martin Buber (1878–1965) is perhaps the best known development of relatedness within the existential therapeutic profession. His work, whilst offering some insights that may be useful for therapeutic practice, has also been profoundly criticised within philosophical circles. Without doubt, the reason for the popularity of Buber's thought amongst therapists is his simple distinction between two forms of relating (I–It and I–Thou) that appear to be directly applicable to practice. This is also, ironically, its fundamental failing, as his over-simplified typology and uncritical romantic language provide an inadequate foundation for a true philosophy of human relations. Nevertheless, many existential therapists find value in his work for the way in which it emphasises two distinctly different types of relating.

The important message of Buber (1923/1958) is that there is no 'I' in isolation. That is, the fundamental starting point for us all – akin to the notion of *Mitsein* in Heidegger's work – is the relationship, between ourselves and other people and also all living things in the world. Within this fundamental relationship there are, for Buber, two distinct ways of relating: with ourselves using only one aspect of our experiencing process (I–It relating) or allowing ourselves to be fully present (I–Thou relating). I–It relating is something readily apparent in much counselling and psychotherapy when we see the client (or patient) treated as an object and the therapist keeping themselves separate from any possibility of a real relationship through a particular kind of professional attitude and quite often the use of techniques. When we see only symptoms of mental ill-health rather than a person struggling to make sense of life, for instance, we fall into the trap of I–It relating. When we set out to cure or remove some individual problematic aspect of experience in a client, then we are also bound to relate to them similarly. This is arguably not always wrong. Many times we might want a medical doctor to simply identify a symptom and treat the disease, with no desire for anything more than this. In therapy, however, this should rarely be the case for the complexity of the human condition demands more than this, and whilst symptom removal may alleviate immediate distress it is unlikely to address fundamental aspects of how to live life better.

I–Thou relating, by contrast, is where we allow ourselves to be fully present to the other and the whole of their experience, and this is the privileged mode of relating for Buber. It is within the *encounter* (or meeting) where such a fundamental aspect of human nature can be witnessed. The encounter is the event or situation where there is recognition of the space between two people or a person and the world and the opportunity for *dialogue*. Dialogue is a loose concept, not specifically tied to language, but is the mode in which we can develop self-knowledge and relate with all other forms of living being. This can be contrasted with technical dialogue and monologue where we speak and listen but do not connect with the other. Silence is also, perhaps paradoxically, essential to true dialogue so that awareness and attentiveness have the space to emerge. Buber (1923/1958) talks of 'being called out of oneself' in such moments and through being truly present becoming a fully attentive human being. The problem with this concept is the vague notion and lack of clarity about what such an encounter truly means, with philosophers such as Kaufmann (1983, cited in Zank, 2007) raising serious concerns about whether this represented a philosophy of relatedness at all or rather an overly romantic (and simplistic) view of relationships, inflected by a particular branch of Hebraic humanism. Whilst this may well be true, and I have seen many therapists who have fallen foul of romanticising the relationship with their clients as a result, at the very least, Buber's work stands as an important reminder of the dangers of treating the other as an object and reminds all therapists of the value of being present and attentive with clients, such that they can come to know them as more than just their presenting concerns or symptoms.

Activity   Think about the relationships in your life, with family and friends, work colleagues, clients and so on, and write a short account of your last meeting. In turn reflect upon each of these meetings, thinking about whether this meeting involved I–It or I–Thou relating. What were the factors involved in determining the particular nature of this meeting? Was this the best way to approach such a meeting in these circumstances? In particular, if you recognise I–It moments, what difference might it have made if you had allowed yourself to be more open to the possibility of an I–Thou encounter?

An interesting development of Buber's thought is the distinction made by Mick Cooper between I–I and I–Me relating (2003, 2004b). Cooper has highlighted the way in which analogous processes to I–It and I–Thou *interpersonal* relating may operate in an *intrapersonal* way, that is, within a person. This development builds on an idea that Rogers expressed in a dialogue between himself and Buber where Rogers suggested that people might have relationships between aspects of themselves (Anderson and Cissna, 1997). Mearns and Cooper (2005: 32) describe these intrapersonal forms of relating as follows:

> The I–I mode is a transposition of Buber's (1958) I–Thou attitude to the intrapersonal level, and can essentially be thought of as self-relational depth. Here a person communicates to themselves – or from one configuration to another – in an empathic and affirming way, recognising different feelings, behaviours, thoughts or configurations as valid and human ways of being ... The opposite of this I–I form of relating ... 'I–Me' relating ... is equivalent to Buber's I–It attitude towards others. Here, the person makes little attempt to 'get inside the shoes' of themselves when

they behaved in a particular way and to understand how they came to act in that manner. Rather, the self, or part of it, is criticised and objectified, or the person may attempt to fully disown that particular way of being.

Cooper (2003, 2004b) sees I–Me relating implicated in a range of psychological difficulties through people for instance, being overly critical of themselves or unable to acknowledge and change problematic aspects of their behaviour towards others. Conversely, he suggests that being able to engage in I–I relating might be thought a definition of good mental health. These ideas are certainly relevant to existential practice and involve a useful shift in analytic focus from the *mitwelt* to the *eigenwelt*.

The third mode of being

Jean-Paul Sartre's views offer a stark contrast with those of Buber, demonstrating a much more pessimistic view of our capacity for equality in relationships. Sartre (1943/1956) thought that Heidegger, whilst recognising that the other was an ontological fact of existence (through the notion of *Mitsein*), failed to provide sufficient evidence for viewing *being-with* as an ontological structure. In order to address this, Sartre (ibid.) described a third mode of Being (that is irreducible to being-in-itself and being-for-itself), *Being-for-others*, adopting his usual strategy of engaging in a phenomenological examination of being as lived. The particular case of shame for Sartre provides evidence for the fundamental existential quality of relatedness. Imagine you are sneaking a look through a keyhole watching someone else. You lose yourself in this moment with no reflective consciousness and the other who is being watched objectified through the *look*. You hear a creak on the stairs behind you as someone approaches and in this moment suddenly become aware of yourself now caught in the *look* of another and become objectified, frozen in shame. This example was, for Sartre, the evidence needed to demonstrate the fundamentally relational nature of consciousness, as shame (like many other states) appears in consciousness immediately through the presence (whether real or imagined) of another consciousness. In shame, therefore, this objectification results in the denial of a person's subjectivity, of their existence as a subject. Sartre thought that this process could, however, be evaded through a similar objectification of the other. This notion of relationality results, therefore, in an unstable dynamic in which people become trapped in perpetually conflictual relationships with others.

> The fact of the Other is incontestable, and touches me to the heart. I realize him through uneasiness; through him I feel myself perpetually in danger. The Other does not appear to me as a being who is constituted first, so as to encounter me later; he appears as a being who arises in an original relation of being with me, and whose indubitable necessity and factual necessity are those of my own consciousness. (Sartre, 1943/1956: Pt. 3, Chpt. 1, Section IV, p. 299)

This is not simply a pessimistic view of relationships, however, but something much more fundamental. Sartre was outlining an ontology of existence in which our fundamental freedom is always at stake. Descartes and other philosophers influenced by his thought had argued that other people were akin to coats and hats and that we had to infer their existence by analogy to our own through behaviour. This fundamental subject–object split was overturned by Sartre, who argued through his example of shame that the other is fundamental to our existence and we know this directly, not by inference, because our own existence would be essentially altered if this were not the case. Human beings, in Sartre's terms, seek to maintain order in the world and control other material objects and this necessarily includes other people. The danger is that we are overwhelmed by the material world and lose our freedom, which is the very essence of what it means to be human. Once we have an awareness of the other being able to judge us and predict our behaviour (as we can see in the example of shame that Sartre evinces), then they become a threat to our freedom and so our response is to seek to control them by reducing them to a thing (destroying their own freedom in the process). This is not a perfect solution to the problem of others, however, as we know that it is not possible to totally reduce the other to a thing. Sartre uses the example of watching a man reading a book with us seeing him as a thing, but through our observation of his reading (and therefore his ability to reflect) we are aware that it is this that distinguishes him from other material things and that he can never be fully reduced to a thing like a stone.

> To remain at home because it is raining, and to remain at home because one has been forbidden to go out are by no means the same thing. It is not mere caprice which causes us often to do, without annoyance, what would have irritated us if another had commanded it. It is because the order and the prohibition cause us to experience the other's freedom as our own slavery. (Sartre, 1943/2003: Pt.3, Chpt. 1, Section IV, p. 294)

Love is not therefore about ownership per se, as has been frequently thought, but a desire to possess the freedom of the other. We are, in a sense, created by the other through their love, as it is their free choice for us that is critical for us to construe our relationship as loving. This leads to a paradox, that whilst we want to possess the freedom of the other and enslave them, we know that without their freedom they could not express their desire for us and constitute the loving relationship that makes them matter so much to us in the first place. Love is, therefore, a hopeless struggle with only three possible positions, which may shift and change dynamically, of course. The first is that a person may become a sadist who seeks to control and possess the other through (symbolic) violence. The second is that a person may adopt the position of the masochist, who allows themselves to be reduced to an object by the other, at the mercy of their will. And the third possibility is to adopt a position of indifference and thus avoid conflict altogether but never fully relate with the other. It is important to note that Sartre was primarily speaking about relationships within the attitude of bad faith here and not of those that might be realised through an authentic stance to the world. Sartre did regard more reciprocal relationships as a (vague) possibility when living authentically with others, though he thought – rather pessimistically – that the majority of human relating was more than likely to be of the kind described above (see Cooper, 1999: Ch. 9, for a good discussion of this).

Activity   When considering the views of Buber and Sartre, which view of relationships most closely resembles your own beliefs about relationships? Think about whether this view is simply a belief that is normal within your culture and history or whether it reflects the way in which you experience your own relationships (these two may not be the same!). Can you see elements of both positions in your relationships or do you see them as fundamentally incompatible? These two contrasting positions highlight a difficulty that all existential therapists will need to face, that of conflicting ideas. Whilst there is a coherent heart to existential philosophy there are very different perspectives on a number of issues, as we see here. This poses a problem for therapists about what to do with these conflicting ideas. Can we work with both? If so, how? Or do we need to make a choice for one and therefore necessarily negate the other? There is no simple answer, but my own view is that there is wisdom in both. This does not mean they can simply be integrated but instead that we may witness moments of both in our work and may therefore draw on these ideas in different moments with our clients.

Gender differences and relatedness

An interesting view on relationships, and in particular the role of gender in them, is provided by Simone de Beauvoir. De Beauvoir (1949/1972) argues that because of gender stereotypes men and women have very different attitudes towards and experiences regarding love. Putting aside the fact that she does not consider same-sex relationships and also noting the historical period in which she is writing, there remains something of interest in de Beauvoir's position. Her argument will probably sound familiar to most people in the West today, with her believing that women become consumed in what she calls *love-religion* whilst men generally treat their love object as a possession, a prize trophy. Furthermore, whilst men want to be loved and may love somewhat in return, loving relationships form only one element of their lives, with other aspects such as work/career, status and so on being in contrast with women who, for a variety of social and economic reasons, give themselves entirely to love. None of this is thought to be set in stone but rather the product of social forces operating differently on men and women in the 1940s, and perhaps at least to some degree even today. Such love-religion is, of course, inherently unstable as the woman has nothing to fall back on and remains in a state of perpetual anxiety at the potential loss of her partner. There is some optimism in de Beauvoir's argument, however, as she believes that when women can love in their strength and not weakness, real love will be possible. Unlike Sartre, she believes that this kind of equal and reciprocal relationship is possible and only hampered by social forces acting to position women differently from men.

Activity   Take some time to think of any of your intimate relationships (whether heterosexual or otherwise) and reflect on whether you think they are founded on equality or some sense of ownership. What are the implications of these different ways of understanding the relationship and would it be possible for your relationships, like that of your clients, to be different?

The fundamental nature of human relatedness

It is with the work of Emmanuel Levinas (1906–1995), however, that we can arguably see the most profound development of a philosophy of human relatedness. There is considerable work to be done in seriously translating his philosophy into practice, but it is worth at least mentioning his radical ideas briefly here. Levinas (1961/1987, 1974/1981) was concerned with the notion of encounter with another person and how this impacts on us like no other object or force in the world. For him, the face of the other calls to us in an emotional way (as an *interruption* in his terms), not even needing to say anything to have power over us. Through rich phenomenological descriptions Levinas, building on Husserl and Heidegger, sought to develop this central idea to produce a truly relational philosophy in which the other is primary, and through this primary relationship explain how language as dialogue emerges. His work has been the subject of some criticism, for instance from de Beauvoir in *The Second Sex* (1949/1972), for what she perceives as his sexism and is now the subject of considerable debate amongst contemporary feminist scholars. It does appear at first glance, however, to speak to the concerns of therapy with a focus on the therapist being summoned to treat the other (a stranger at first) as the primary concern in the dialogue that follows. Beyond this there is undoubtedly much more in this work of relevance to therapy and this is surely something that will be realised in due course by those seeking to develop a sense of relational ethics within existential therapy.

Spinelli (2007) provides an interesting account of the implications of our fundamental relatedness for the practice of counselling and psychotherapy. Spinelli describes four distinct *inter-relational realms*: the *I-focussed*, *You-focussed*, *We-focussed* and *They-focussed*. The I-focussed realm concerns the client's experience of him- or herself within therapy, for instance 'I am feeling sad' or 'I always have this happen to me because ...'. The You-focussed realm involves dispositional expressions directed to the other (the therapist), such as 'You understand me' or 'You don't know what it is like for me'. The We-focussed realm involves that which occurs between client and therapist and concerns the inter-relational ground which also exists in I- and You-focussed realms but is more implicit there. Expressions emerge from either client or therapist and might include statements such as 'it seems like we are struggling to understand each other right now' or 'we really have made progress here'. And finally, the They-focussed realm concerns the client's experience of the wider world of others (extending beyond the people directly engaged within the therapy room) and include statements such as 'my mother never tries to understand me' or 'I always struggle to be nice to my work colleagues but they just take advantage of me'. There is some similarity in Spinelli's description of these four realms with the four dimensions of existence outlined in Chapter 6. His focus appears to be on highlighting the need for the therapist to ensure that the They-focussed is not lost within the therapeutic encounter and his relational typology offers a potentially useful way of interrogating the work going on in the here-and-now with a client. A beginning therapist, in particular, might find it useful to be aware of what is occurring during therapy in the light of these distinctions and reflect on what that says about the therapeutic process. Spinelli suggests that an examination of the They-focussed realm may be particularly useful in enabling a client to realise the fundamentally relational nature of life and see how they are enmeshed with the other people in their world. Clients may tend to talk in one realm more than another and, as can be seen with the four dimensions, an absence of talk within one or more of these realms may be revealing about the way the client is engaged at that moment with the issue of concern. A lack of talk within the They-focussed realm may, in particular, highlight a lack of responsibility on the part of the client for their choices and relationships with others. Spinelli rightly points out that it is not the therapist's role to act as judge here, or attempt to force a client to be more responsible, but he argues that 'the existential psychotherapist cannot avoid raising these inter-relational issues since *the whole of the therapeutic process has been, and continues to be, an investigation of relatedness*' (2007: 184, italics in original). That is, for Spinelli (and I tend to agree), exploration of the implications of client change for others within their relational realm forms as central a part of the therapeutic process as an examination of the emotional or cognitive life of the client.

Case study   Rachel

Rachel came to see me because of the anger she was feeling with her boyfriend. She would rage at him and felt that this was out of control. They had been together for seven years but she felt increasingly frustrated that he was unable to meet her needs. I spent considerable time trying to understand what Rachel felt was lacking, and it seemed as if it was his inability to comfort her appropriately when upset that was the crucial lack. At first this seemed relatively straightforward, with them having simply become complacent around the relationship. However, when I explored other relationships in Rachel's life a pattern emerged. It appeared that she felt let down by all the people in her life in the same way. Was this that she was unfortunate with all those people she knew, from her parents and siblings to partner and friends, or did she have a role to play in this? It seemed unlikely that everyone was failing her, though I did not rule out this possibility. With further discussion I felt that Rachel would constantly shift the goalposts with her needs, moving from wanting someone who would simply listen to wanting someone who would take charge. Whenever I offered a challenge to this effect she would subtly correct my understanding of her needs. I was continually wrong-footed and myself felt unable to meet her needs. This was particularly telling, so rather than working hard to examine her relationships I instead focussed on trying to meet her needs in therapy as best I could. This involved a lot of support though I could not be passive, as this too would feel like rejection to her. With time our relationship became stronger and stronger and I could once again offer up some challenges concerning her own role in her situation. With the trust that had developed between us and her own increasing confidence about being able to have her needs met, by me at least, she started to recognise that she needed to work on what she expected from others. This was a long slow process, with many ups and downs, but a productive one. This work could not be done quickly as time was essential to enable her to trust me and for me to understand how I could respond appropriately to her needs as they arose in the therapy. But over time things improved with her partner as she came to realise what he was offering her.

Further reading

Buber, M. (1923/1958). *I and thou*. Edinburgh: Clarke.
  A very accessible introduction to Buber's thought. Just be careful not to get seduced by the evangelical tone.

De Beauvoir, S. (1947/1976). *The ethics of ambiguity* (trans. B. Frechtman) New York: Kensington.
De Beauvoir, S. (1949/1972). *The second sex* (trans. H. Parshley). Harmondsworth: Penguin.
  Two classic texts by De Beauvoir, both of which are remarkably accessible.

Peperzak, A. T., Critchley, S. & Bernasconi, R. (Eds) (1996). *Emmanuel Levinas: basic philosophical writings*. Bloomington: Indiana University Press.

A good compilation of essays by Levinas, with useful introductions and notes from the editors.

Sartre, J.-P. (1943/1956). *Being and nothingness: an essay on phenomenological ontology* (trans. H. Barnes). New York: Philosophical Library.

Another classic that is not easy going but another 'must read' for the aspiring existential therapist.

Spinelli, E. (2007). *Practising existential psychotherapy: the relational world*. London: Sage.

An excellent account of Spinelli's approach to existential therapy, which is strongly grounded in a relational model of existence. Indeed, it appears that for Spinelli relationality is the heart of existential therapy itself.

NINE   Emotions and Embodiment

CHAPTER AIMS

This chapter aims to:

- provide an introduction to two key aspects of existential therapeutic practice: emotions and embodiment;
- explain how ideas about these philosophical concepts can be applied in practice;
- provide a number of case studies to show the value of these different concepts in different therapeutic situations.

Emotions

As discussed in Chapter 3, the notion of *attunement* from Heidegger (1927/1962), and how all of our experience is through Dasein's *mood*, is central to existential therapy. At the ontic level we experience moods as feelings and they offer clues to how people are experiencing their world, what matters to them, even if this might initially be out of conscious awareness. Emotions are, therefore, central to existential practice and much of our work involves us attending carefully to feelings being expressed or not by our clients and/or responding to presenting problems around feelings (whether this be sadness, anxiety, jealousy or anything else). For instance, extreme levels of sadness (traditionally characterised as depression), in Heideggerean terms, involve a person being closed off to beauty and joy in the world. Sadness is not therefore some intrapsychic conflict but rather a constrictive view of the word. Our role in therapy is to attend phenomenologically to what is being embraced in the world (pessimism in relationships, for instance) and what is being closed down (the opportunity for a relationship to strengthen us and expand our world, for instance). With time clients may be able to see this for themselves (for it is no use us simply pointing it out) and as a result begin to open up their worlds. Key to change is to work phenomenologically with the client, offering up challenges where appropriate so that they are able to gain insight into what is being closed down in their world and, given the will, effect change. A number of existential philosophers and therapists have developed theories of emotions beyond Heidegger, and below I briefly elaborate on these ideas and discuss their applicability to therapeutic practice.

Sartre's (1939/2002) *Sketch for a Theory of the Emotions* presents an intriguing, though not entirely comprehensive, theory of human emotions. He first considers existing psychological theories of the time when he was writing, including that of William James, Pierre Janet and Tamara Dembo, before moving on to outline his own ideas. The starting point for Sartre is that emotions, like all other aspects of consciousness, are intentional (in the sense I discussed previously in Chapter 2). They are, therefore, directed towards some object and cannot be considered separately from the object to which they are directed. We always engage with the world and the objects within it in a particular emotional manner and a full understanding of what this means requires that we consider both our emotional state and that to which it is directed. Further to this, Sartre highlights how life involves getting things done and, as a result, we experience things as means or obstacles to achieving what we wish. To this end, we construct what Sartre refers to as a *hodological map* (from the Greek *hodos*, meaning path or pathway), which is, in effect, an imaginary map of the pathways by which we seek to achieve our goals. The consequence of experiencing the world through such an emotional hodological map is that we treat the world as if it were an artefact of our own. It is when problems emerge in us following our expected route through our hodological map that emotions arise as we attempt to magically transform the world. That is, we do not recognise and accept the limits being placed upon our wishes by the world but instead act as if we are able to transform it magically. Of course, this is futile but not something that we do reflectively but is rather simply part of our consciousness of the world itself and how we experience it. Sartre in typical style provides a number of illuminating examples to provide evidence for this theory and with these we can see how this theory makes sense, at least when considering disagreeable emotions (though not so much with emotions that we find agreeable). The most persuasive example is that of suddenly seeing a face at the window of our home and being gripped by terror. At this point, the world is not available to us for what we can do with it, with us able to reflect rationally on what is possible or not for us. Instead, we see the world in magical terms and scream or faint in order to make the face, the threat, the fear disappear from our view. Similarly, we might see a bunch of grapes up high on a vine and reach out for it whereupon we realise that we cannot reach them. At this point, we simply dismiss the grapes as being unripe and not what we wanted anyway. Emotion is then an inferior mode of consciousness in which our capacity to engage in the world in terms of its utility for us disappears and is replaced instead by a magical alternative.

> **Activity**   Think about a recent time when you felt yourself in the grip of some powerful disagreeable emotion. Upon reflection do you think you moved from a practical mode of consciousness to a magical one as a result of some frustration to your hodological map? Now do the same when thinking of some agreeable emotion and ask yourself whether Sartre's theory of emotions makes the same sense here.

Eugene Minkowski (1933/1970) also developed some significant ideas about how we might come to understand depression from an existential perspective. The key for understanding this particular emotional condition is time and the way in which the relationship between past, present and future may break down. Minkowski argues that depression occurs as a result of a person being unable to see a future whilst simultaneously confronting *existential guilt* for their past. Existential guilt is where a person feels that they have not lived up to their own potential. This can sometimes be the result of unrealistic aspirations or a mismatch between goals and ability, but regardless it can often be paralysing. Defences mobilised to ameliorate such existential guilt may include myths about ourselves or the world we inhabit (if only I had got the break like others I would have been a success), and within existential therapy it may be necessary to gently confront the way in which such defences perpetuate an unrealistic way of living tinged by existential guilt. The inability to see future possibilities and potential is resonant with the ideas of Heidegger, who similarly stresses the need for the past and future to be incorporated into the way life is being lived in the present. Successful therapy can not simply occur, therefore, by looking to the past for answers but needs to be focused on present understandings necessarily inflected by past experience and future possibilities.

It is frequently the case that clients presenting for therapy are stuck in their existential guilt, defended through elaborate myths about themselves and the wider world and *sedimented* beliefs (Merleau-Ponty, 1945/1962). Over time and often through habit certain beliefs and consequent actions will become *sedimented*, fixed like the sediment in the bottom of a bottle. It is common amongst people feeling depressed that we see sedimented beliefs and actions that only serve to reinforce such beliefs, resulting in a vicious spiral. For instance, a person may come to believe that no one in the world cares for them and they feel down as a result of this sense of isolation and abandonment. But instead of going out in the world and trying to find someone who does care (and thus challenge their belief), they will withdraw from people, hide away and so never allow the possibility that their belief be challenged. It is important to attend to such things in therapy and when appropriate working with the client to find the courage to test their own belief system out in the world.

Strasser (2005) makes an interesting distinction between reflective and unreflective emotions. His concept extends Sartre's (1939/2002) ideas about emotions but Strasser argues that emotions may be expressed in a reflective way as well as the unreflective manner described by Sartre. He explains that for Sartre unreflective emotions depend on an immediate rapport between subject and object, with awareness of moving us beyond the 'magical spell' cast by the emotion we are experiencing. Strasser quite rightly points out that Sartre's conception of emotions works pretty well for 'negative' emotions such as fear, anger or disgust, but seems to fail when we examine more 'positive' emotions such as joy (see Fell, 1965, for criticism of Sartre's position here). Strasser explains that for other writers emotions only emerge when reflected upon (see, for example, Lewis, 1993) and it is for this reason, alongside his own experience of therapeutic practice, that Strasser believes – quite rightly in my view – that we need to consider emotions in both their unreflective and reflective modes of expression. As such, one of the aims of therapy is the active exploration of both reflective and unreflective emotions. Clients frequently present because they feel their emotions are out of control ('I cannot stop myself from getting angry at my children') and want help to remove a troublesome emotion. It is, of course, not possible to do away with a primary emotion, but when such unreflective emotions are reflected upon there is an opportunity for the therapist and client to examine the total context of the emotional life of the client, with the possibility that the client may gain greater control over their emotional world. Emotions may also emerge unreflectively within the therapeutic process, and once again it may prove fruitful to work with the client to bring awareness of these emotional responses into reflective consciousness.

Finally, it is worth mentioning Deurzen's (2009) notion of the emotional compass (see Figure 9.1), which is a particularly useful way of conceptualising our emotional life from an existential perspective. In the emotional compass Deurzen has different types of emotions in different positions around the circle, with those reflecting depression, disappointment and

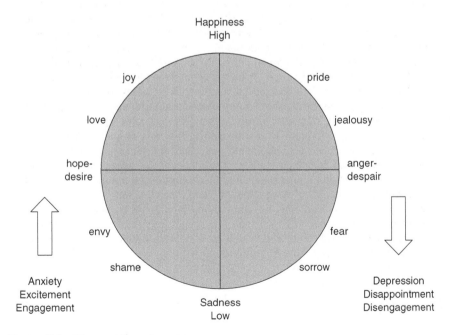

Figure 9.1 The emotional compass

Source: Reproduced from Deurzen, E. van (2009). *Psychotherapy and the quest for happiness.* London: Sage.

disengagement pointing south and those reflecting anxiety, excitement and engagement pointing north. The idea with the compass is that we move endlessly around it, with some people occasionally becoming stuck in one particular quadrant. This way of thinking about our emotions is undoubtedly useful in practise as we attend to the nature of the emotions being expressed, thinking through their relationship to other emotions and how these feelings might be driven by anxiety and engagement or by depression and disengagement. The compass emphasises the way in which we all cycle through different emotions from moment to moment and how certain emotions may cluster together or be opposed to each other through their relationship to anxiety and depression.

Case study   Sara

Sara came to see me following the break-up of her relationship with her partner. She had broken up with partners previously and was puzzled by why she felt so 'out of control' with this one. She suffered from crippling bouts of depression and could not understand what was going on. When I first met Sara I was struck by how in control she appeared within the session, and this continued throughout the early sessions. A great deal of her life sounded as if it was under total control and anything less was inappropriate for her. She did not drink alcohol for fear of being out of control, for instance. With some investigation it became clear that this latest break-up threw her in two ways. First, she did not feel sure that she wanted the relationship to end when it did (unlike her previous relationships), even though she had ended it herself. Second, her partner met someone else very quickly after they broke up, moved in with them and began to talk about formally registering their partnership and having children. This had been something Sara wanted and it seemed as if her very tight hodological map was under threat, with emotional turmoil the result. The sense of control over the world that Sara sought was unsustainable and in our work she came to realise this. She also came to see why control was so important. She grew up in a household that was on the surface terribly respectable and proper but underneath was filled with tension as both parents drank excessively. She had played down the impact of this aspect of her past but came to link it herself with her own need to be in control of her world. Sara started to test out the possibility of living differently, and whilst this was very scary for her it also proved to be rewarding. I supported her through her experiments in living and felt enormous pride in how bravely she sought to engage in the world. With time her 'lows' became fewer and the impact of her loss integrated into a new and revitalised sense of self.

Embodiment

Emotions are, of course, a key aspect of embodiment as they, like all other aspects of our existence, work through our bodies. There is much more to the body than emotions alone, however, and issues of embodiment have been considered in considerable depth by a number of important existential thinkers. Heidegger (1987/2001: 321) thinks that 'the bodily [*das Leibliche*] is the most difficult [to understand]', in spite of his belief that it was the foundation for all being-in-the-world. Indeed, in much analytic philosophy there has been a notable lack of work that has focused on the body or treated it seriously. However, existential philosophers since Nietzsche have always been keen to stress the way in which experience is embodied, with these issues taken up in earnest by a number of philosophers including Maurice Merleau-Ponty, Jean-Paul Sartre and Simone de Beauvoir. I briefly outline some of the key existential ideas here before moving on to consider some more contemporary philosophers who have also critically addressed issues of embodiment, gender and sexuality from an existential perspective.

Sartre devotes a chapter to the body in *Being and Nothingness* (1943/1956). Whilst his views have been criticised by Merleau-Ponty, who arguably developed the most sophisticated existential view of embodiment, it is worth briefly outlining Sartre's thoughts here. Sartre (ibid.) distinguishes the *body-for-itself*, our own experience of our bodies, from the *body-for-others*, the way our bodies appear to others and their bodies appear to us. Further to this, we have the recognition that how I experience my body is distinct from how others see my body (what Sartre refers to as the third ontological aspect of the body). The body-for itself and the body-for-others are ontologically distinct categories, with our bodies not reducible to one or the other. The body-for-others is most clearly understood as the body of medicine. When consulting a medical doctor there is a sense of handing our body over as an object to the critical interrogation of medicine. Our experience of our body is likely to be part of the picture when our medical history is being taken, but our bodies are then treated as an object to be examined. Another person can never know what it is like to live in my body and likewise I can never know what it is like for them. Instead, we have an objectifying gaze between us as we look upon each other and only by analogy come to bridge this gap.

Merleau-Ponty discusses the body at length in *Phenomenology of Perception* (1945/1962) and also in his last unfinished work *The Visible and the Invisible* (1964/1968), and in the process develops the most sophisticated account of embodiment within the existential canon. Merleau-Ponty's entire philosophy implicates the body through the *body-subject*. The notion of the body-subject stresses the way in which all consciousness must be understood through our bodies, their relationship with other bodies and the world they inhabit. Merleau-Ponty's target was the dualism of traditional philosophy: mind–body, self–world, inside–outside. His philosophy sought to provide an alternative, one which is grounded in the primacy of our bodies for all understanding. Any suggestion that one could doubt the existence of our bodies, as Descartes did, is utterly inconceivable for Merleau-Ponty, as thinking cannot exist beyond the body-subject. Our bodies are not objects separate from consciousness but the means by which we engage with the world; all consciousness stems from our embodied position in the world and, therefore, the world only makes sense through an understanding of it through the notion of the body-subject.

A further important element in how our bodies cannot be thought of as objects like other objects in the world concerns the way in which we do not need to decide what our body should do through conscious reflection. As I sit here typing I am conscious of the words that I wish to write but do not then need to instruct each finger to move to the appropriate key on the keyboard, they move effortlessly to where they are required. The example of sport exemplifies the point most clearly. A good tennis player does not consciously think about their place on the court, position of the racquet and so on but responds almost apparently without thought to what is required. In such situations there is not the time for reflective thought, and indeed any such reflective thought may interrupt embodied action and disrupt the free flow of movement. This is more significant than it may at first appear. As Merleau-Ponty (1945/1962: 153) states: 'whether a system of motor or perceptual powers, our body is not an object for an "I think", it is a grouping of lived-through meanings which moves towards its equilibrium.' This position runs counter to much philosophy, including some existential philosophy, which emphasises the notion of subjectivity that is founded on will and deliberative action and instead emphasises something more basic, an embodied *practical* subjectivity that is fundamentally in relation with the world. Habit, whether the habit of knowing where to place one's fingers on a keyboard or where to move to on a tennis court, is not simply something that is mechanistic but is 'knowledge in the hands, which is forthcoming only when bodily effort is made, and cannot be formulated in detachment from that effort' (Merleau-Ponty, 1945/1962: 144).

Merleau-Ponty's work on embodiment was taken yet further in his last incomplete work, where he offers up a tantalising philosophical vision that has inspired many contemporary philosophers. Merleau-Ponty (1964/1968: 136) moves his focus from embodied consciousness and the body-subject to inter-corporeal being, what he termed *flesh*: 'the world is at the heart of our flesh ... once a body-world relationship is recognised, there is a ramification of my body and a ramification of the world and a correspondence between its inside and my outside and my inside and its outside.' He uses the example of touching to demonstrate the double belongingness that is central to life. If we touch our left hand with our right hand when one hand is touching (that which is perceiving), then the other hand is touched (that which is the object of perception) and vice versa. This double belongingness is represented in Merleau-Ponty by his notion of the *chiasm* (from 'chiasma', the crossing over of two structures) and is not reducible (to one hand or the other) but represents an inextricable relationship between body and world, with each folded into the other. Our subjectivity, as embodied, is never located, for instance, in either being touched or in touching but in the dynamic intertwining of both. This idea of a merging of body and world is difficult to grasp as it runs counter to much of our everyday thinking about our bodies, bounded by their skin and their separateness from the world they inhabit. Merleau-Ponty argues that we need to move beyond this dualistic way of thinking and instead recognise the way in which body and world are inextricably intertwined. The feminist phenomenologist Iris Marion Young (1985: 30) in her discussion of pregnancy provides a vivid example of such intertwining: '[Pregnancy] challenges the integration of my body experience by rendering fluid the boundary between what is within, myself, and what is outside, separate. I experience my insides as the space of another, yet my own body ... [But also] the boundaries of my body are in flux. In pregnancy, I lose the sense of where my body ends and the world begins.'

Gender and sexuality

Gender and sexuality have been somewhat neglected topics in philosophy, until relatively recently at least, but within the existential tradition there have been some important contributions to these topics. De Beauvoir (1949/1972), of course, took the issue of gender as her central theme in *The Second Sex* and through her focus on women's experience highlighted the issue of sexual difference, which remains a major issue in contemporary writing on feminist theory. Sexual difference was mostly ignored by de Beauvoir's contemporaries, with more recent feminist scholars criticising Heidegger, Sartre and Merleau-Ponty for this neglect (see, for instance, Le Doeuff, 1991). Feminist criticism stems from the argument that these male existential thinkers produced universal theories that are applicable to both men and women. On this basis, one might question whether such theorising is possible or whether it neglects important differences between men and women, and their embodied experiences. It is only women, for instance, who can experience pregnancy. Furthermore, there have been additional criticisms that the supposedly universal theories developed by, for instance, Sartre are in fact theories founded on (and therefore only applicable to) male experience (Le Doeuff, ibid.). Feminist scholarship has consistently highlighted this tendency in much psychological and psychotherapeutic work by male writers, basing their theories on men's experience (neglecting women's experience) and assuming that this is universal. Much of the power of de Beauvoir's work is how it highlights the impact and importance of sexual difference through a detailed phenomenological analysis of women's experience. This is, of course, itself historically and culturally situated and must be understood in that light, but we are still far from equality between the sexes or indeed free from the influence of sex and gender on our experience, if that is ever possible or even desirable.

Young (1990), writing in the 1970s, draws on Merleau-Ponty and de Beauvoir in her well-known essay *Throwing Like a Girl*. In this essay Young discusses the reasons why, in general, girls and women throw differently to men. Young starts with the fundamentals by considering how, if differences in throwing were attributable to muscular differences, women should be expected to throw in a style similar to men, given that this style of throwing is more effective, putting more of their bodies into their throwing action and maximising throwing capacity. She then points out that in fact nearly all of women's physical activities (whether running or hitting) do not make the most of the body's spatial and lateral possibilities. Young argues that this is an example of the way in which the socio-cultural is represented through people's bodies, rather than being the effect of any 'natural' biological differences. That is, as a result of socio-cultural expectations around sex and gender, women are more inhibited at a bodily level than men, more wary and hesitant of their own bodies. Women see themselves through the eyes of others more than men and as a result objectify themselves and therefore are more self-reflexive than men: there is a bigger gap between mind and body for women than for men. Of course, this argument was first made in the 1970s and things have undoubtedly changed, but nevertheless it highlights the power of the social world and the way in which it directly impacts on all aspects of our being-in-the-world. Grosz (1994) takes this argument to a new level, recognising changing social circumstances, but staying with the idea that women's bodily experience remains different from that of men. She uses the example of women having breasts and how the way in which they are subjectively experienced and how they are objectified is clearly very different for men than women. The consequence of these arguments is that the attempts at universal understandings of embodiment (that we see with Sartre and Merleau-Ponty) need to be tempered with an understanding of the way in which sex/gender, and indeed any other aspects of embodiment that may be inflected by socio-cultural factors (such as age, race/ethnicity, dis-ability, sexuality and so on) impact on the experience we have of our bodies and more generally our place in the world.

Merleau-Ponty (1945/1962) also provides an important account of sexuality in *The Phenomenology of Perception*. Unlike many previous writers (such as Freud), Merleau-Ponty does not see sexuality as a drive but rather as a modality of existence, an essential part of being a body-subject. For him, sexuality infuses every aspect of existence, being part of our situation in the world. This runs against much contemporary thought about sexuality, and also many commonplace assumptions, which are invariably inflected with a psychoanalytic notion of sexuality as drive (like hunger) that propels us towards certain actions. In order to evidence his assertions, Merleau-Ponty discusses a well-known neurological case study of a man named Schneider, who demonstrated some puzzling behaviours. Using this case Merleau-Ponty identifies key differences between sexual desire and hunger, and on this basis argues that sexuality needs to be understood differently, as a perceptual phenomenon that is intentionally bound to the world. Sexual response is not a reflex but rather another aspect of intentionality, bound up with the meanings we ascribe to other people and objects in the world.

More recently, Ernesto Spinelli (1996), has attempted to develop an existential theory of sexuality. He emphasises the 'chosen' nature of sexuality and draws on Isay's (1989) arguments about gay children experiencing a sense of 'otherness' to extend this idea to heterosexuality. Whilst Spinelli (1996) is persuasive in his arguments against a bio-reproductive basis for human sexuality and his desire to bring sexuality into contemporary existential practice laudable, I believe that he over-emphasises the role of social forces in the construction of sexualities. Whilst a person may choose their sexual identity, this choice is not equally clear or easy, particularly if the sexuality one is choosing is condemned by the social world into which one is thrown (Heidegger, 1927/1962). The 'otherness' described by Isay may be experienced by heterosexual individuals if, for instance, they express particular dissident sexualities (such as a sado-masochistic sexual identity). However, by and large, their heterosexuality is the 'ground', rather than the 'figure', in their sexual being-in-the-world, much as masculinity is the ground for gender. That is, it is rarely reflected upon or critically interrogated but instead simply operates as the norm, imbuing those who manifest this sexual identity with considerable privilege and cultural capital.

This is not the case with lesbian, gay or bisexual (LGB) identities (let alone trans [T] identities), where feelings of otherness require a decision to confront or deny that which the individual discovers and/or creates in him- or herself. Nor is this decision a simple or easy one when an individual finds him- or herself in a world in which people are routinely condemned for expressing the very same sexual identity. The impact of heterosexism and homonegativity on people who are lesbian, gay or bisexual is well-documented (see Ritter and Terndrup, 2002). These attitudes have an adverse impact on the psychosocial development of lesbians, gay men and bisexuals (much as gender normativity does on trans people). The negativity associated with prejudice can be internalised and directly turned against the self, even in the absence of an external aggressor or oppressor (Malyon, 1982). This internalised homonegativity has also been conceptualised as a universal developmental outcome for lesbians, gay men and bisexuals (Shidlo, 1994).

In light of these socio-cultural factors, it is unrealistic (and perhaps even unethical) to expect an LGB or T client to do all of the work of countering such prejudice alone. The impact of the social world on clients and their perception of their sexuality or gender cannot and must not be underestimated. The therapist is in a uniquely privileged position to have a direct impact on the world of another person in an affirmative way. Through the direct affirmation of LGB and T identities, therapists can work with clients by helping them to resist the external and internal homo negativity, alongside gender normativity, that they inevitably encounter (see Langdridge, 2007a, for more on this and the possibility of a gay affirmative existential therapy).

> **Activity**   It is important for therapists to be reflective about their own body, gender and sexuality and comfortable in dealing frankly with these issues in a non-judgemental way as they arise in therapy. Spend some time reflecting and then writing about your own body, gender and sexuality. Consider the following questions when you write: Are you happy with your body and issues of gender and sexuality? Do you understand and feel in control of your gender and sexual desires? – always or sometimes? Were you brought up in a family environment where it was acceptable to discuss your body, gender and sexuality? Are you comfortable with others discussing issues to do with your or their body, gender and sexuality? If not, what makes you uncomfortable?

It is worth mentioning, albeit briefly, the absence of discussion about other key aspects of embodiment amongst the existentialists, notably race and ethnicity. In a sense this is partly a result of the writers being a product of their time, though this is no excuse for their failure to engage with such important issues. To be fair, Sartre and de Beauvoir (along with others like Camus) did discuss matters of race in their writing and engaged directly in many political campaigns of their period. They were key intellectual contributors to many important political campaigns in their era and undoubtedly had a profound impact on the social world of their time. In terms of their writing, Sartre's (1948/1995) discussion in *Anti-semite and Jew* of the nature of racism is notable, and a book worthy of attention, if far from perfect in it's analysis of this particularly troubling cultural phenomenon. There remains, however, a serious lack of writing in which differently raced bodies are discussed in terms of their specificities, and this is something that is in need of remedial attention.

In the terms described above, attending to embodiment becomes an important element of therapeutic practice. Whilst we may be engaged in a 'talking cure', there is much more to existential therapy than simply talking about things in a detached way. Not only must we attend closely to emotions, we must also recognise the way in which the bodies of our clients alongside our own body are inextricably bound up in the experiencing process. Issues of embodiment may come to our attention in therapy in very obvious ways (see the case study below, for instance) when a client presents concerns with some aspect of their body (such as their weight) or when suffering from an illness that directly impacts on their body. Ideas from Sartre can be particularly useful here for helping us to unpick the ways in which present concerns reflect our own understandings of our bodies and their objectification by others. However, what Merleau-Ponty alerts us to is the way in which issues of embodiment cannot be detached from any other aspect of experience. All experiencing occurs through the particular body that is having that experience, and this undoubtedly frames the way in which such experience becomes understood. There are many opportunities in therapy to reflect on these issues and bring in aspects of embodiment ourselves, even when it does not appear to be the primary presenting concern. Finally, de Beauvoir and Young remind us of the need to situate all bodily experience within a wider social context. The body-subject is inextricably bound up in the social world into which it is thrown (as flesh) and has this self-same social world folded into it. Sex, gender, sexuality and all other aspects of our embodied experience (such as race/ethnicity) need to be understood within the particular history and culture in which such bodies are situated. As therapists seeking to help others and effect change in the world, we forget this crucial issue at our peril. If we wish to take the phenomenological heart of existential therapy seriously we must, of necessity, recognise the way in which all experience, which is always embodied experience, is situated in a particular history and culture, which will inevitably allow and limit our understanding of the meaning of such experience.

Case study   Will

Will came to see me as he felt that his life was over. He had been living with HIV for over 20 years, taking anti-retrovirals on and off for many years though now needing to adhere to the medication to keep himself well. He was single and had been for the last 11 years and felt there was no chance that anyone would want to be with him. He was very angry with the world and spent many of the early sessions ranting about whatever matter was concerning him (whether it be the death of the planet or parking tickets). During these periods I was unable to do much other than listen. In time we established more of a dialogue and became able to explore his central concern, which was his loneliness and feeling that no one would want to be with him. Much of this revolved around his appearance and sense of being a pariah. In spite of him living with HIV for so long it appeared that he had never really come to terms with his diagnosis. He had faced considerable stigma early on when the medication he was taking led to severe lipodystrophy, with friends abandoning him and others shunning him on the basis of his appearance. He carried the scars of his experience with him now in spite of him now showing very few outward signs of his infection. Will objectified his own body, separating it from his sense of selfhood, as he spoke. He saw his body through the eyes of others or the medical profession and I never saw any sense of the body-subject or flesh in his conscious reflections. We focused in on his body and how he felt soiled, with me allowing him the space to describe himself thus but never being complicit in doing this myself. I very gently suggested that there might be other ways of understanding the impact of this illness and also challenged him that others would simply write him off. I encouraged him to attend a support group for long-term survivors of HIV, and this offered him some comfort and also critical challenge to his taken-for-granted assumptions. Throughout our work I needed to be careful to allow him the space to voice his self-hatred but balance this with warmth and care. I also needed to be mindful of the practical reality of living with HIV, the physical and emotional consequences of drug treatment and the continuing stigma surrounding this illness. There were some signs of progress, with Will occasionally being more positive about himself and the prospects of someone else wanting to be with him, but he cut short our work together as he decided he 'had had enough of talking about this fucking disease', and I only hope that he managed to continue to find ways of living constructively with his illness.

Further reading

De Beauvoir, S. (1947/1976). *The ethics of ambiguity* (trans. B. Frechtman). New York: Kensington.
De Beauvoir, S. (1949/1972). *The second sex* (trans. H. Parshley). Harmondsworth: Penguin.
    Two classic texts by De Beauvoir, both of which are remarkably accessible.

Grosz, E. (1994). *Volatile bodies: toward a corporeal feminism*. Bloomington: Indiana University Press.
    A superb book by an important contemporary philosopher and social theorist, drawing on a very wide range of philosophical sources which place the body and, in particular, gender and sexuality centre stage.

Langer, M. (1989). *Merleau-Ponty's phenomenology of perception: a guide and commentary*. Basingstoke: Macmillan.
    An excellent guide to the phenomenology of perception, which takes the reader through Merleau-Ponty's work chapter by chapter.

Merleau-Ponty, M. (1945/1962). *Phenomenology of perception* (trans. C. Smith). London: Routledge.
Merleau-Ponty, M. (1964/1968). *The visible and the invisible* (trans. A. Lingis). Evanston, IL: Northwestern University Press.
    Two classic texts that are a 'must read' for any existential therapist. Not easy going but well worth the effort.

Sartre, J.-P. (1939/2002). *Sketch for a theory of the emotions* (trans. P. Mairet). London: Routledge.
    An excellent little book from Sartre, very accessible though limited in its scope. Certainly not the whole story as far as understanding emotions is concerned, but still an interesting development.

Strasser, F. (2005). *Emotions: experiences in existential psychotherapy and life*. London: Duckworth.
    An interesting book in which Strasser discusses the role of emotions in therapeutic practice, with case studies providing examples across a range of emotions that might be commonly seen in practice.

Young, I. M. (1990). Throwing like a girl. In *Throwing like a girl and other essays in feminist philosophy and social theory*. Bloomington: Indiana University Press.
    Very interesting feminist philosophy drawing on Merleau-Ponty and De Beauvoir. The other essays in the collection are also well worth reading.

Part III

Extending the Theory and
Practice of Existential Therapy

Part III

TEN   Researching Existential Therapy

CHAPTER AIMS

This chapter aims to:

- provide an introduction to some of the issues involved in researching existential therapy and briefly outline existing evidence in support of this therapeutic approach;
- discuss the differences between outcome and process research;
- outline the range of phenomenological research methods that are particularly relevant when researching existential therapy.

This chapter begins by briefly discussing the role of research in counselling and psychotherapy before moving on to discuss different types of research, including the differences between outcome and process research. After this I look at the specific context of existential therapy and briefly discuss challenges in researching existential therapy and existing literature on this orientation. There is, unfortunately, a relative dearth of literature on existential therapy but what there is provides some interesting insight into the value of this therapeutic perspective. There is not the space in one chapter to provide a thorough introduction about how to conduct research, but I hope that there will be enough here to form the foundation for any reader wishing to start the journey to becoming a practitioner-researcher. Finally, the phenomenological method has been drawn on by a great deal of academic work in psychology and I briefly outline the different types of phenomenological research that are commonly employed and their particular applicability to investigating existential therapy.

Researching counselling and psychotherapy

Conducting research is somewhat alien to many counsellors and psychotherapists, with many practitioners indifferent to research findings of relevance to practice and/or the possibility of conducting research themselves. This situation is changing fast as a consequence of external requirements for evidence-based practice and a general 'up-skilling' of the profession (Rowland and Goss, 2000). There is a growing consensus that practitioners need to be aware of research relevant to their work, and students on counselling and psychotherapy training programmes now often need to conduct small research projects themselves. Beyond this there have always been people who have straddled the research–practice divide, fulfilling both academic research and practice roles. Research can at first glance appear difficult or beyond the skill set of counsellors and psychotherapists, but this is very far from the truth. In fact, many of the skills vital for effective practice are directly transferable to the realm of research.

Activity   Spend some time reflecting on your own thoughts about research. Write down what you think research is all about and your thoughts about its relevance to counselling and psychotherapy. Try to think of as many examples as you can of the reasons for therapists reading about or conducting research themselves.

There are many reasons why therapists should read about research and also conduct it themselves. Without research we cannot know whether what we are doing is actually effective. Whilst we gain invaluable knowledge through practice itself there is enormous value in getting evidence beyond our own, necessarily limited, experience to validate our beliefs in the value of what we do. Beyond this, there is also the need to know that the form of therapy that we conduct works as well as or better than other forms of therapy. To date, this knowledge is somewhat lacking for existential therapy. Through research we can also come to know what works best for particular groups of people with particular presenting concerns, and also learn more about what it is that we do which works best. Without research it is very difficult to know what it is about the process of therapy that clients find of most value, and we have an ethical obligation to our clients to ensure that we pay serious attention to their needs and meet them with the best evidence-informed practice that we can.

Cooper (2004a), writing specifically in the context of existential and humanistic therapies, offers another intriguing reason for the value of research for practitioners. He argues that research offers the opportunity for challenge to our assumptions and beliefs about our therapeutic practice. Research in these terms acts as deconstruction and challenge, providing independent evidence (for instance, from clients themselves) that we can use to examine our own work. This is particularly valuable with existential therapy where empirical research can help avoid the risk of running wild with philosophical abstraction, losing sight of the everyday concerns of the client. Research in these terms provides a space for thinking critically about our work and in the process become more adept and open practitioners.

Quantitative and qualitative research

An important distinction can be made between *quantitative research*, concerned with quantities or measurement of phenomena (counting, invariably involving statistics) and *qualitative research*, concerned with the quality or qualities of some phenomena (often meanings). Quantitative research remains the dominant approach in the UK and much of the rest of the world today. Quantitative research tends to be based upon a particular empirical approach to knowledge that is often thought to be at odds with some varieties of counselling and psychotherapy, existential therapy included. Quantitative research tends to be characterised by a number of factors above and beyond the simple use of quantification and measurement. Attempts are generally made to control influences beyond the target variable of interest to increase precision, often by conducting research in tightly controlled environments, such as laboratories. There is also often a focus on prediction, based on studies with large numbers of participants, rather than simply description, and the testing of hypotheses. Within counselling and psychotherapy research, quantitative research is most often associated with outcome research (see below).

Qualitative research by contrast is principally concerned with understanding what something means to people or the way in which it is constructed through language, often by recording and then transcribing verbatim what was said in an interview or – within this field – perhaps a therapy session. Qualitative analysis tends to focus on working closely through transcribed text in order to ascertain meaning or, in some methods, the way in which language is being used to achieve something (like justifying a person's position). Work tends to eschew any notion of testing a hypothesis (prediction) and instead focus on description with the possibility that unexpected insights into phenomena may emerge. Qualitative research also tends to draw on small numbers of people, unlike most quantitative research, and has generally been used more for process research (see below) than outcome research within counselling and psychotherapy.

You will note that throughout the above paragraphs I have spoken about these distinctions using words such as 'tends' or 'generally', as there are always exceptions to these categorisations. It is also worth noting that there has been considerable growth in mixed methods research, where both quantitative and qualitative methods may be used (see Langdridge and Hagger-Johnson, 2009: Ch. 24, for more on this). Employing mixed methods research designs is not without difficulties or tensions, however, and beginning researchers should be careful when contemplating such designs. In general, qualitative methods, particularly phenomenology (see below), have been the perspective of choice in existential therapeutic research. These methods are clearly more aligned with the spirit of existential therapeutic practice and the focus of engaging phenomenologically with clients, such that we can come to understand the way the world appears to them.

This is not to say that it is not possible to employ quantitative approaches, and indeed there are arguments that we need more quantitative outcome research within the field.

Outcome, evaluation and process research

There are many different types of research, with one important distinction for counselling and psychotherapy research being that between outcome and process research. *Outcome research* is primarily concerned with investigating the efficacy of therapy: whether it works or not. The aim of outcome research is attempting to understand how a particular therapeutic intervention has helped a client, for instance through the reduction of symptoms. There is a long tradition of research focussing on the outcomes of therapy, particularly that concerned with the question of whether therapy works or not. There is now considerable evidence to support the belief that therapy in general works (see Cooper, 2008, for an excellent review). That is, we know from research that therapy in general is an effective intervention to help people deal with the issues in life that we all must face from time to time, whether that be anxiety, sadness or any other psychological challenge. Barkham describes four generations of outcome research (noting that he includes elements of process research alongside) and also provides an invaluable introduction to this research tradition. The four generations of research are, in brief, concerned with: (1) whether psychotherapy is effective and whether there are objective methods for evaluating process; (2) which psychotherapy is more effective and what components are related to outcome; (3) how we can make treatments more cost-effective and how change occurs; and (4) the clinical significance of therapy for the individual (Barkham, 2003: 27).

In order to determine whether therapy has been effective, or indeed what kind of therapy is more effective, it is first necessary to have a way of measuring outcomes to see what impact the therapeutic intervention has had on the client. There are numerous measures, mostly in the form of questionnaires, for a very wide variety of possible clinical symptoms, from depression and anxiety inventories to general health and well-being measures. Perhaps the most well-known measure that has been adopted by very many services in the UK is the Clinical Outcomes in Routine Evaluation – Outcome Measure (CORE-OM), which comes in a variety of forms and can be downloaded free from www.coreims.co.uk (correct at the time of writing). The CORE-OM is not tied to any therapeutic orientation or focussed on a single presenting concern but is instead a general measure appropriate for many therapeutic outcome studies, incorporating questions designed to tap anxiety, depression, general functioning, physical problems, trauma and risk.

Whilst CORE-OM is a good generic outcome measure in widespread use, it is important to note that no single measure is appropriate for all clients or all research situations. There are many other *valid* and *reliable* measures designed to assess therapeutic outcomes (such as the Beck Depression Inventory and the Generalised Anxiety Disorder instruments). *Validity* refers to whether the instrument measures what it claims to measure (so a high score on a depression questionnaire should occur with a person who would be clinically diagnosed with depression) and *reliability* refers to the consistency of measurement (a person who is depressed should come out with similar scores on the measure if they complete it more than once). We use established measures, rather than creating our own questionnaires, for these very reasons: we know that they are valid and reliable as they have been tested previously and there will also be norms for these measures against which we can compare people.

Once outcome measures have been selected the next key element of this kind of research is the study design. There are many possible ways of designing an outcome study but there are a few common designs in regular usage. One of the most important issues concerns the use of a *control group* when carrying out outcome research. If, for instance, we simply asked clients to complete a measure like the CORE-OM before and then again after therapy we have no knowledge of what else might be contributing to any changes in scores obtained before and after. A person may have an improved score but this may be as a result of other factors in life, such as starting a new relationship or being given medication by their doctor, intervening rather than anything that occurred in therapy. Indeed, it may simply be a case that over time things tend to get better and so the person would have improved their scores regardless of whether they attended therapy or not. It is, therefore, necessary to control for these factors and this is where a control group comes into play. A control group consists of a group of people (ideally selected in a similar manner to those attending therapy) who receive no therapeutic intervention during the study period. So, we would have two groups in our study, one receiving therapy for a specific period and the other receiving no intervention at all. Both would be tested at the beginning and then again at the end of the study period (and possibly several times in between). One of the best ways to operationalise a control group is to have a waiting list group who will eventually receive the therapy but whilst waiting have no intervention.

The 'gold standard' is generally thought to be the *randomised control trial* (RCT) in which people are randomly allocated to one of the two conditions (receiving therapy or not receiving therapy). Random allocation of people to the two groups minimises the potential for bias so that any differences that are found between the two groups in their outcome measures can be attributed to the therapeutic intervention. RCTs were designed for drug trials in medicine (comparing the efficacy of a new drug with a dummy drug, a *placebo*) and whilst they can be used to a certain extent for therapeutic outcome research there are some problems. An important element of the RCT is that the study should be *double-blind*. That is, neither the

participant nor the researcher should know which condition the participant is in. This is because it has been shown that simply knowing which
condition one is in will have an impact on the person, and this can even
be influenced in very subtle ways by the researcher knowing who is in
what condition. Needless to say, it is not possible to conduct a full double-
blind study when researching counselling and psychotherapy outcomes as
the therapist must know what treatment is being administered, since they
are doing it, and the client knows they are receiving therapy rather than a
dummy intervention. Instead, compromises need to be made with RCTs
though they remain a very important source of information in assessing
the efficacy of different forms of therapies.

Evaluation research is sometimes indistinguishable from outcome
research, though there is a distinct tradition of work within the therapy
field concerned with investigating particular interventions, often at the
level of organisations: 'Evaluations are concerned with whether or not
programs or policies are achieving their goals or purposes' (Berk and Rossi,
1990: 15). Evaluation research can be large scale, investigating a new
national initiative, or small scale, investigating the work of just one practitioner. Evaluations may also be formative or summative, with the former
designed to feed back and enhance the design of ongoing interventions and
the latter designed to provide a definitive evaluation of an existing service.
Evaluation research is generally seen at the level of organisations and so
invariably involves consideration of both practical issues and the political
implications of the work. It is beyond the scope of this chapter to discuss
evaluation research further but there is a comprehensive literature which
provides comprehensive guidance. Barkham and Barker (2003) provide a
useful introduction with references to the important literature in the field.

Process research, on the other hand, is concerned with how therapy
works, with a focus on understanding the therapeutic elements involved in
client change. The work of Rogers (the founder of client-centred counselling) and his colleagues represent some of the first systematic studies of
process within counselling and psychotherapy (Rogers, 1942, 1951, 1961).
Their work was concerned with the process of change within clients and
also the client–counsellor relationship. Through the analysis of recordings
of sessions they were able to investigate client change in self-concept
(perception and acceptance) to see how this was related to successful outcomes. Their work demonstrated the value of a phenomenological
approach to therapy research, where the experience of clients was prioritised
and also led to Rogers' own development of his client-centred approach
to counselling.

There are a number of different methods for conducting process
research, though one of the most significant today is the *events paradigm*
(Rice and Greenberg, 1984). The aim is to focus on change events
within therapy sessions and identify actions conducted by the therapist
that led to this change. This can be distinguished from the older – though

still important – tradition of work which involves examining more general conditions or processes involved in effective therapy associated with the early pioneering research of Rogers and his colleagues discussed above. The *interpersonal process recall* (IPR) method has proven to be a particularly valuable tool in this body of work (Kagen, 1984). Here, a therapy session is recorded (using video or audio) and then played back to either the client or therapist or both. This is designed to stimulate recall of the session experience so that client and/or therapist can then comment on what occurred in the session within a recorded research interview. Insight can, therefore, be gained into what was helpful or into significant events that led to change (Rice and Greenberg, 1984; Mahrer et al., 1987). This technique has yet to be utilised within existential therapy, at least within the published literature, but offers much promise for providing greater insight into what aspects of our therapeutic practice are helpful and might facilitate change.

A final body of work on process has specifically focussed on the client's experiences. Clearly, it makes a great deal of difference if research is conducted on therapists' or clients' perceptions of the experience of therapy (see Yalom, 1989, for a fascinating account of the different experiences of client and therapist). Research has, for instance, been completed on the experience of clients following completion of counselling as well as the experience of clients over extended periods of counselling (see, for instance, Maluccio, 1979), with other work conducted on single sessions using IPR (Rennie, 1990). Rennie (2002) and Cooper (2008) both provide useful reviews of such client-focussed studies.

Case study research

Writing case studies will be a familiar experience to all trainee and experienced therapists alike. *Case study research* draws on the process of describing detailed individual cases, using them as a research tool to understand more about the key elements in therapy. Case study research began, of course, with the work of Freud and his now classic case studies of Dora (Freud, 1901/1979) and the Rat Man (Freud, 1909/1979), known by most therapists. This tradition of research continues to this day amongst psychoanalytic practitioners but has also been taken up by therapists of other orientations as a way of communicating interesting insights into the therapeutic process. Aside from this tradition of case study research there also exists work known as 'N = 1' research studies, particularly within behavioural therapy research ('N' is used in research studies to specify the number of participants). With this approach, studies tend to track a single case using repeated measures of behaviours (such as time spent engaging in problematic behaviours or depression inventories) to see if and when change occurs (see Morley, 1989). Within the existential tradition the former is more common, though unlike psychoanalytic work there is little that has been published in peer-reviewed journals. Most case studies from an existential perspective appear as illustrative material in books like this one, though there are some examples using this method in existential and humanistic journals (see the following section for information on relevant journals).

Another method worthy of mention is the *hermeneutic single-case efficacy design* developed by Elliott (2002), which combines elements of both outcome and process research within a single case study design. The method outlined by Elliott is complex but comprehensive, incorporating both quantitative outcome measures, records of therapy sessions, alongside a qualitative change interview. The aim with this approach is to rule out other possible reasons for change occurring with a single case. To this end, Elliot describes an approach involving the triangulation of multiple sources of information. Whilst complex and requiring considerable effort on the part of the investigator, it is a method that does not need extensive resources and can be conducted on a small scale by an individual therapist-researcher, perhaps working in partnership with another therapist-researcher. There is considerable opportunity for existential therapists to conduct research of this kind and with sufficient trials the possibility of building up a substantial body of research evidence.

Research study   Brian – a critical narrative analysis

Here I provide a summary of a piece of research I carried out myself (see Langdridge, 2009). The work represents a novel attempt to carry out case study research with one of my own clients in a way that clearly separates my clinical work with the client from a research interview and consequent phenomenological narrative analysis. In this piece of research I conducted a narrative style interview with a longstanding client. This required considerable thought and care to ensure that the client's needs were prioritised throughout but also proved rewarding both in terms of contributing to our understanding of a much maligned issue and also with our therapy.

Brian came to see me as he was struggling with a relationship he had formed within the context of his desire to live as a 24/7 sadomasochistic (SM) slave. Sadomasochism is a much misunderstood sexual practice/identity, still unfortunately pathologised by many working within the mental health professions (though see Langdridge and Barker, 2007, for a different perspective). Our therapeutic work had been ongoing for 14 months when I approached Brian at the end of a session to ask if he would be willing to take part in a research interview. I asked him to take his time and think about it and emphasised that he was, of course, able to say 'no' with no effect on the therapy. In fact, one of the important reasons for selecting Brian, apart from his fascinating life story, was because I felt confident that he would be able to say 'no' should he want to. As it happens, he was eager to take part and we arranged a research interview separate from our regular therapy sessions. I adopted a phenomenologically informed narrative approach to the interview and analysis (see Langdridge, 2007b, for more on this). It consisted of asking one question about his life story as it related to his interest in SM and then an analysis of the narrative structure and content of his account. What emerged was the way in which his life story concerning relationships was, in many ways, similar to many others in spite of it being inflected with a masochistic slave sub-text. His account was clearly split into two narratives: before meeting his Mistress and after meeting his Mistress. Before he met his Mistress he would visit professional dominatrices and was continually engaged in a search for fulfilment, which was never achieved, of his sexual identity as a slave. After he met his Mistress he discovered the possibility, in a real, concrete and emotional way, of a permanent realisation of his identity through a loving SM relationship. The second narrative shifted from a classic story of 'romance' to one of 'tragedy' as personal issues resulted in this relationship breaking up, which prompted him seeking therapeutic help. His story and the move from control (when visiting professional dominatrices), uncertainty to self-realisation was akin to the 'coming-out' stories of lesbians, gay men and bisexuals. Ultimately, it was his inability to see himself as 'good enough' to warrant a loving SM relationship that led to the emergence of his insecurities and subsequent difficulties in maintaining such a relationship, something that is common to many people struggling with relationships of any type. Not only was the research productive in terms of understanding more about SM but it also fed back into the therapy, serving as a valuable meta-review session. The close attention paid to the transcript of the interview and analysis also proved valuable for me as a therapist in bringing back otherwise lost elements of his story, enabling me to highlight quite how much progress he had made in his journey.

Existential therapy and research

There are some people within the existential therapeutic tradition that believe that there is no place for research. I think this is wrong. Within such arguments we inevitably see two things: research understood only in terms of a particular kind of quantitative outcome research (for instance, comparing the efficacy of existential therapy with another therapeutic approach on some quantitative outcome measure, such as a depression scale) and also mysticism of the existential approach (often wrapped up as creativity/diversity). Let's take these two things in turn. The first concerns what we understand by therapeutic research. There are many different types of research (discussed in more detail in the section on outcome and process research above) but so often when arguments are forwarded against researching existential therapy a very particular kind of research is conjured up: randomised controlled trials concerned with quantitative outcome measures of therapeutic efficacy. This is the stuff of drug trials, for instance, when we see two groups of people (randomly selected to each group) given a new drug or a placebo (a dummy drug like a sugar pill), with the key things being whether those who receive the drug improve in some way (cured or their symptoms alleviated) that is statistically differently from those that received the placebo. Even here there is scope for existential therapy to be included in such research trials, though we do need to acknowledge the limitations of such studies in the context of therapies that cannot readily be *manualised* (reduced to a specified set of techniques that can be consistently applied by different practitioners). The second argument about existential therapy is, in many ways, more worrying. There is a tendency amongst some existential therapists to position this particular form of therapy as a form of esoteric practice in which it is impossible to specify what may or may not constitute good practice. As I mentioned above, this is often wrapped up, none too subtly, as the need for individual creativity and diversity. Whilst there is undoubtedly a need for creativity and diversity amongst existential therapists, this is no different from the creativity needed by a humanistic, gestalt or psychoanalytic therapist. As I hope I have shown in the previous chapters, there is a core to existential therapy that must form part of practice for anyone seriously wishing to use the label. Whilst the philosophy that underpins this therapeutic orientation is often rather obtuse, there needs to be clarity about its translation into therapeutic practice. Mystical statements about what occurs in therapy, accepting that there is much we do not understand, do ourselves a disservice but more importantly do our clients a disservice and, at worst, act as a cover for a lack of insight into our own way of working and resistance to embracing the value of research for improving practice.

As mentioned at the beginning of this chapter there is relatively little published research specifically focussed on existential counselling and psychotherapy (see Walsh and McElwain, 2002, for one of the most comprehensive reviews of research on existential therapies published to date). In the UK some small-scale work continues to be published in the journal of the Society for Existential Analysis (*Existential Analysis*), though much of this is not of the same scale or quality as that produced for other therapeutic orientations. There is also a substantial 'grey' literature that has yet to be fully examined or exploited which stems from graduate student dissertations in existential therapy training centres. Many masters and doctoral students have conducted research of value, but this has often not been sufficiently exploited through publication in academic and professional journals. Yalom (1989) provides some direct evidence in support of the existential approach, but one of the most significant recent contributions to knowledge comes from work in a form of experimental existential psychology known as *terror management theory* (TMT) (Greenberg, Koole and Pyszczynski, 2004).

TMT is based on the idea that there is a biological predisposition to survive, to continue to exist, and that this fundamental fact of life leads to the development of human strategies designed to ameliorate the terror of death. It is the cognitive abilities of human beings to comprehend the finite nature of life that leads to this uniquely human response to the threat of death. The primary mechanism through which terror is managed is self-esteem and the notion that one has an important place in a meaningful universe. For this to be effective it is necessary to share a cultural world-view, alongside a belief that we are meeting the standards of that world-view (self-esteem). It is quite obvious how this work has been driven by fundamental existential ideas about being-towards-death, amongst others. The intriguing element of this theory is how researchers have tested these ideas using cleverly crafted experiments. Many hypotheses have been generated concerning the way in which we need to maintain self-esteem as a buffer against anxiety generated through our fear of death and how inducing a sense of our own mortality will lead to strategies designed to uphold particular cultural worldviews and self-esteem. There is now substantial empirical evidence in support of TMT and consequently in support of fundamental ideas from existentialism (see Greenberg, Koole and Pyszczynski, 2004, for an excellent summary). This work continues and forms an important body of knowledge in support of existential theories and also provides further empirical insights into the way in which these ideas underpin so much of our behaviour.

However, perhaps the greatest extent of research relevant to the practice of existential therapy comes from the academic tradition of phenomenological psychology, studies of humanistic therapy (sometimes indistinguishable from existential therapy or at the very least inflected with existential ideas) and also generic counselling and psychotherapy research. Cooper (2008) provides an excellent overview of generic counselling findings, much of which makes sense within an existential therapeutic perspective. There are also a number of key journals which publish relevant research, though to date no one has published an adequate review of the many disparate findings of direct relevance to existential therapy; thankfully this is something that Professor Mick Cooper at the University of Strathclyde is currently working on with his colleagues Joel Voss and Meghan Craig. Important journals include: *The Humanistic Psychologist, Journal of Humanistic Psychology, Journal of Phenomenological Psychology, Indo-Pacific Journal of Phenomenology* and *Person-Centred and Experiential Psychotherapies,* alongside other more generic journals in counselling, psychotherapy and psychology. Whilst it is unlikely that funding will be obtained for large-scale outcome or process research on existential therapy, there is still an opportunity for us all to find creative ways of contributing to knowledge. What is urgently needed is for existential therapists to ensure that they review existing work from within and outside our tradition and then engage in research themselves with the aim of publishing their work in reputable journals for others to read and build upon. Only then will we be able to stand alongside colleagues from other orientations in an equal manner, for whilst the ideas underpinning existential therapy are undoubtedly persuasive, without empirical evidence from good-quality research we will struggle to convince others (whether potential clients, colleagues, other healthcare professionals, possible employers and so on) of the value of our work.

Phenomenological research methods

Phenomenological research methods are well established within a number of academic disciplines and, perhaps not surprisingly, offer one of the most appropriate sets of tools for researching existential therapy. There is a family of phenomenological methods rather than one single method, with distinct differences between the ways in which research is conducted from each family member (Langdridge, 2007b). These differences invariably stem from the various strands of phenomenological philosophy being drawn upon by those who have developed each method, but all share a common focus on understanding experience. I believe that phenomenological methods can be broadly categorised into three groups: descriptive, interpretive and narrative. It is worth noting that others categorise the range of phenomenological methods somewhat differently. Finlay (2011), for instance, separates the field into six groupings: descriptive empirical; hermeneutic; lifeworld; interpretive phenomenological analysis (IPA); first-person; reflexive-relational. Whilst another valid way of categorising the field, and there is much to be said for acknowledging such subtle differences, I see enough similarities between hermeneutic, lifeworld, IPA and reflexive-relational methods to put them all within the broad category of 'interpretive methods', given that they all tend to draw on the same philosophical foundations. I also do not see first-person work as a distinct methodological tradition but rather as a different, and somewhat controversial, way to collect data within an interpretive phenomenological framework. I discuss each of the three groupings in turn below before discussing the value of them for research in counselling and psychotherapy.

The earliest explicitly formulated phenomenological method is that of *descriptive phenomenology*, most notably associated with the pioneering work of Amedeo Giorgi and colleagues at Duquesne University, USA in the 1960/70s (see Giorgi, 2009). This approach is also sometimes referred to as 'the Duquesne school', 'empirical phenomenology' or 'Husserlian phenomenology', and a considerable body of work has developed building on the foundational work of Giorgi. It is strongly grounded in the philosophy of Husserl, staying close to his principles, although also informed by the work of other philosophers like Heidegger. The aim is to engage in description of concrete experiences in order to identify the essence of the phenomena being explored. Sample sizes are small, recruited through maximum variation sampling (attempting to get people from different backgrounds who share the experience). This is so greater confidence can be gained in identifying a common core to the phenomenon being studied. Data is generally collected through written concrete descriptions and/or through unstructured or semi-structured interviews. The epoché and phenomenological reduction are taken seriously as part of this very rigorous method. Whilst there are variations and developments, the core of descriptive phenomenology remains clear: a focus on concrete experiences that are then subject to an analysis designed to identify the essence of the phenomenon, whilst also accounting for variant properties. Although this group of methods are the most established, they are relatively unknown in the UK, though still used widely in North America and elsewhere in the world.

The second major grouping of phenomenological methods are *interpretive* or *hermeneutic phenomenological* approaches. There are some notable variations amongst this group of methods but in general there is more interpretation than might be seen with descriptive phenomenology, producing a thematic description of the essence of the phenomenon. Some of these approaches still engage seriously with the epoché and reduction whilst others transform this into a form of reflexivity. The work of Karin Dahlberg and colleagues (2008), Linda Finlay (2011; Finlay and Evans, 2009), Max van Manen (1990), Jonathan Smith and colleagues (2009) and Les Todres (2007) best exemplify this tradition. The influence of the philosophies of Heidegger and Gadamer can be more clearly seen with this group of methods, though they still have their roots in the phenomenology of Husserl. Data tends to be collected through semi-structured interviews, transcribed verbatim and then analysed thematically. Sample sizes remain small and these are generally homogeneous and purposive, with an attempt to minimise variation. In general, there is more thought about the way that meanings emerge through language, and also on the relationship between the researcher and participant. The common core, however, is a focus on developing a rich thematic account of a common experience. There is more awareness of these methods within the UK than those of descriptive phenomenology, with a particular focus on their use in applied areas of psychology where they have proven to be tremendously popular.

The final group of phenomenological methods to note are *narrative* approaches. Some authors do not consider these as part of the family of phenomenological methods but I do for there is a distinct tradition of narrative research that is heavily indebted to phenomenological philosophy and works very clearly within this philosophical framework. The work of Dan McAdams (1993), myself (2007b, 2009) and Donald Polkinghorne (1988) best exemplify this tradition of phenomenological work. This work is strongly influenced by the hermeneutic philosophers Gadamer and Ricoeur, though particularly the latter. The fundamental principle is that our understanding of the lifeworld is mediated through language and, in particular, the stories we tell of our experience. Data is collected through life-story or occasionally unstructured or semi-structured interviews, transcribed and then analysed in terms of the stories that underpin accounts of experience, often including account of features such as narrative tone and function. Narrative research, in general, has grown in popularity in recent years, though this has been somewhat slower within the phenomenological tradition than amongst other forms (such as that informed by discourse analytic principles). However, there are attempts, such as my own, to advance ideas in phenomenologically informed narrative methods, and increasing numbers of people are coming to recognise the value of this group of methods.

Whilst I have drawn distinctions above about the forms of phenomenological methods commonly employed today, it is important to note that there are many overlaps and commonalities that may be obscured by this categorisation. There are also many examples of work that have not been mentioned in this all too brief section; notable omissions include the considerable number of people who have advanced work in phenomenological research methods such as Chris Aanstoos, Peter Ashworth, Scott Churchill, Steen Halling, Bernd Jager, Ernest Keen, Steiner Kvale, Jim Morley, Clark Moustakas, David Seamon, Adrian van Kaam, Fred Wertz and many more besides. What is important is to understand the place of each method within the broad philosophical tradition that underpins the field, alongside the need to acknowledge the considerable work which has already been undertaken by others to advance phenomenological research methodology. There is no right or wrong method but varieties of method within the phenomenological family that speak to different concerns that researchers might have. There is still much more to be done and there are some obvious areas where phenomenological researchers need to focus their attention, but phenomenological research methodology is broad and rich and of tremendous value for anyone wishing to conduct research within counselling and psychotherapy that is both respectful and insightful.

Phenomenological research methods have an obvious appeal to existential therapists and undoubtedly should be the method of choice for many researching within this field. There remains a lack of work on existential therapy directly that is published in good-quality journals, however, and my hope is that more and more existential counsellors and psychotherapists will seek to address this problem. What is also important is that beginning researchers work systematically to build new knowledge. This requires a systematic review of the literature and then the formulation of appropriate research questions that are focused on illuminating experience as lived. Too often I see student work that pays scant regard for what has already been conducted on their topic (a very quick look through some of the journals in the field would alert them to this immediately) and also that fails to do justice to the varieties of phenomenological methods that we have on offer. Different methods suit different research questions and it is important, therefore, that before beginning to conduct a phenomenological study the beginning researcher takes the time to examine the broad family of phenomenological methods. With care taken in both planning research and conducting it as well as possible, we have the potential to build an invaluable body of knowledge within this profession that not only informs practice but also contributes more generally to the greater sum of knowledge that we have about the human condition.

Research study   Men's experience of loss

There has been a dominance of stage theories of grieving over the last 40 years, in which it is expected that people will work through discrete stages of mourning and recovery, but these have more recently been the subject of considerable criticism. In a small phenomenological study based in Denmark, Spaten, Byrialsen and Langdridge (in press) sought to investigate bereavement amongst three men, all of whom had experienced the loss of their partner to cancer. There has been relatively little research that has focussed on the experience of men suffering bereavement and the work was prompted by this, alongside our own experience of working psychotherapeutically with men who were struggling to come to terms with the loss of loved ones. Attempts were made to recruit a larger sample of men but this did not prove possible, in line with other research that has struggled to recruit men experiencing bereavement. Regardless, the hermeneutic phenomenological analysis proved to be insightful, even if we must be tentative about the findings, and of potential value for other therapists working with men experiencing bereavement. Three essential themes emerged from the analysis: 1) grief and self-reflection, 2) meaning of life and loss, and 3) re-figuring the lifeworld. There was no sense of working through discrete stages for these men but rather a complex emotional response with them moving rapidly between anger, grief, meaning and meaninglessness. Anger was particularly potent for these men, mixed with a myriad of others feelings. The importance of social sharing was emphasised, along with the need to re-figure their identities in the light of their loss and changing circumstances. A 'one size fits all' approach to offering bereavement services was clearly inappropriate, for whilst there were commonalities in the experiencing process there were also key individual differences. For instance, for two of the participants having children and now 'having to be both a father and a mother' to their children forced them to continue to engage with life immediately in the aftermath of their loss. And whilst the other participant had a longer struggle to return from the depths of despair he found a way to make sense of his loss and similarly find a way to grow as a human being as a result. There was no sense of letting go for any of the men but rather a process of employing strategies to help them face life again and find new worthwhile identities for themselves.

Further reading

Barkham, M. (2003). Quantitative research on psychotherapeutic interventions: methods and findings across four research generations. In R. Woolfe, W. Dryden & S. Strawbridge (Eds), *Handbook of Counselling Psychology* (pp. 25–73). London: Sage.

   A superb introduction to quantitative research in counselling and psychotherapy with comprehensive references to other sources of information on outcome research. Chapter 4 on evaluation research is also a valuable starting point for interested readers.

Cooper, M. (2008). *Essential research findings in counselling and psychotherapy: the facts are friendly*. London: Sage.
    An excellent book providing an overview of research findings for counsellors and psychotherapists. A 'must-read' book for all therapists offering considerable insight into effective practice.

Finlay, L. & Evans, K. (Eds) (2009). *Relational-centred research for psychotherapists: exploring meanings and experience*. Chichester: Wiley-Blackwell.
    Excellent coverage of many of the issues involved in qualitative research within counselling and psychotherapy. It also includes a number of exemplar chapters, including one of my own developing a phenomenologically informed critical narrative approach to research in psychotherapy.

Langdridge, D. (2007). *Phenomenological psychology: theory, research and method*. Harlow: Pearson Education.
    My own book on phenomenological research methods. In this book I provide both theoretical and practical advice on the range of phenomenological methods commonly employed today.

Langdridge, D. & Hagger-Johnson, G. (2009). *Introduction to research methods and data analysis in psychology* (2nd edn). Harlow: Pearson Education.
    This book provides a broad overview of both qualitative and quantitative research methods. It assumes no prior knowledge and takes the reader through the basics of conducting (psychological) research, including the variety of qualitative methods along with quantitative methodology and the statistical analysis of data.

McLeod, J. (2003). *Doing counselling research*. London: Sage.
    Another excellent book providing tremendously useful information on conducting research for counsellors.

Walsh, R. A. & McElwain, B. (2002). Existential psychotherapies, in D. J. Cain and J. Seeman (Eds), *Humanistic psychotherapy: handbook of research and practice*. Washington, DC: American Psychological Association.
    The best review of research on existential counselling and psychotherapy published to date.

ELEVEN   Power, Politics and Language

CHAPTER AIMS

This chapter aims to:

- provide an introduction to some key developments in existential thera-py, including the roles of power, politics and language in contemporary practice;
- explore the place of power and politics within existential therapy and high-light one possible way to address the need for an appreciation of power and politics within existential practice;
- discuss the way in which language and particularly the stories clients tell of their experience need to be taken seriously and appreciated within the broader social context in which they live;
- provide a number of case studies to show the value of attending to lan-guage, power and politics within existential therapy.

In this final chapter I introduce and discuss some contemporary develop-ments in the theory and practice of existential therapy. Whilst the previous chapters have outlined the core of this particular therapeutic approach, it is vital that we do not stand still, stuck in a particular historical period, when attempting to understand the worlds of our clients who, like us, are living in continually changing circumstances. Furthermore, any discipli-nary tradition must remain critically engaged with developments within and outside the discipline and seek to renew itself continually. There is a dangerous tendency in much counselling and psychotherapy – and existen-tial therapy is no exception – to act as if we have the answers to effective practice and need do nothing more than apply our ideas, concepts or tech-niques consistently. It is crucial that all therapists engage in continuous professional development, and this should be taken seriously. This does not mean that we need to seek out ideas from other forms of therapy and become eclectic therapists but rather that we cannot simply assume that all the answers can be found in Heidegger or Sartre. These ideas and their translation into practice certainly provide the core of existential therapy and should not be discounted or abandoned in search of something better or new, but there is always space to develop these ideas further, particu-larly their application to practice, whilst remaining true to the spirit of existential therapy. This chapter seeks to do just that and highlight some key areas (primarily concerning power, politics and the role of language in therapy) in which a number of people, myself included, have sought to develop the theory and practice of existential therapy in recent years. I end this chapter, and indeed the book, with a discussion about the future of existential therapy. I believe that the future of existential therapy lies in us all working to continually advance theory and practice. If this form of therapy is to survive, and indeed flourish, then we all need to embrace the critical dynamism at the heart of existentialism and continue to think critically about the theories and practices of our chosen therapeutic orientation: retain the core whilst also pushing boundaries.

Existential therapy, power and politics

The relationship between counselling, psychotherapy and politics is a complex one. Many counsellors and psychotherapists, existential therapists included, pay scant attention to issues of power and politics, preferring to assume that by adopting their particular therapeutic methodologies the therapeutic space is neutral or apolitical. Indeed, such an apolitical stance is a particular danger for existential therapists given that the phenomenological method has little to say about politics, on a macro level at least. For many existential therapists politics enters the therapeutic space through the lifeworld of clients only at an individual level, with the therapist and the broader social world bracketed out of any direct political engagement. A client may therefore raise political issues but by adopting a rigid phenomenological stance many existential therapists will not engage directly but rather simply seek to understand the struggles of the client. This is not necessarily a bad thing, and a wise therapist will be careful to move beyond this stance. However, there are some therapists who have gone further and who seek a more direct and practical engagement with the political.

The work of Andrew Samuels (1993) is a notable example of a therapist seeking to both use their therapeutic knowledge to engage in political discourse and also allow space for the political to influence their practice. Samuels works from a depth psychology (principally Jungian) perspective, but his mission is worthy of serious attention by all therapists, regardless of orientation. Samuels makes the persuasive point that there is a need to bridge the private (clinical) and public (political) domains in our work and that both are enriched by this possibility. We cannot escape the political no matter how much we engage phenomenologically with our clients, as both client and therapist are necessarily situated within a broader political world, within particular ideological positions. A refusal to acknowledge this leads only one way, towards the conservative as we abdicate our responsibility and deny our power to effect change.

On a personal level, I am driven to explore the possibility of addressing the political in therapy directly and have sought to do this by drawing on the hermeneutic philosophy of Ricoeur alongside critical social theory (see below). This has come about as a result of my own experience as a gay man living in these late modern times and the experience of working with clients who have suffered oppression. When I hear the struggle of a gay man in his forties to accept himself or the struggle of a young black woman in the face of homonegativity and racism respectively I am moved to act. Their stories resonate with me on a deeply personal level and my overriding desire to effect change at a broad political level is brought to the fore. Bringing the political directly into the therapeutic space requires considerable care, however, and is not something to be done lightly. Better a therapist stick rigidly to the phenomenological stance than act recklessly, imposing their own will on their clients. But I do believe we have a duty, an ethical duty to acknowledge our power, gained through our position as professionals to offer something that is finely tuned to the clients' situation, bounded as it is by their place in the socio-political world we all inhabit.

I find it ironic that existential therapists, of all people, should eschew direct political engagement. Many of us have found a home amongst the existentialists as a result of our dissatisfaction with the status quo, our desire to live a better life and our critical stance on so many taken-for-granted assumptions. The existential philosophers that have given rise to this form of therapy similarly expressed a desire for change and their philosophical enterprise sought to do just that.[1] However, whilst many existential philosophers were passionately engaged with politics on a personal level, their philosophical writing so often leads to crass political individualism and a failure to directly engage with broader social issues. There are some notable exceptions, including de Beauvoir's work on sex and gender and Sartre's (1960/2004) later engagement with Marxism in his *Critique of Dialectical Reason*. There have, however, been few attempts to draw on this work or move beyond existential thinking on the political within existential therapy itself. There is much to do if we are to bridge the gap between the private and public, to engage our power to effect change, to work harder to enable our clients to live their lives as they wish, free of the limits of an oppressive social world.

Ricoeur (1988, 1992) was a notable exception within the broad existential tradition for the way in which he attempted both to outline an ethics (as we also see with Levinas) and engage directly with politics in his work on ideology and utopia. In *Oneself as Another*, Ricoeur outlines his 'little ethics' whilst also developing his ideas about narrative identities and in his (1996) *Lectures on Ideology and Utopia* he attempts to bring theories of ideology and utopia together under one overarching conceptual framework (see Langdridge, 2005b, for the possible application to conflict and reconciliation).

---

[1]Noting, of course, that for some of these philosophers political engagement has unfortunately – and rather ironically – been fascistic rather than focussed on opening-up possibilities for all.

In common with all his work, he seeks to bring together previously opposed positions in a way that does not reduce one to the other. In the following section I briefly outline developments in hermeneutics and focus in on how we might use some of Ricoeur's ideas to better work with language, power and politics directly within existential therapy.

Hermeneutics and the possibilities of working with language, power and politics

Psychotherapy, in all its incarnations, is an exercise in *hermeneutics*. Hermeneutics concerns the ways in which we come to understand through interpretation. The shift in phenomenology from the descriptive project of Husserl to a hermeneutic (interpretive) one in Heidegger signals the turn to hermeneutics within existential psychotherapy. As mentioned earlier in this book, Heidegger did not abandon the phenomenology of Husserl but instead sought to recognise the way in which all understanding is historically and culturally situated and thus in need of interpretation to grasp the meaning of the world for us: a hermeneutic project. As human beings we are continually engaged in a hermeneutic project as we go about our lives. We seek to make sense of the world we inhabit, and this requires that we engage in an interpretive sense-making process. Similarly, the psychotherapist must act similarly when engaged with a client, attempting to understand the sense-making activities of the client. Two figures within the hermeneutic philosophical tradition stand out and have particular relevance for developing the theory and practice of existential therapy: Hans Georg Gadamer (1900–2002) and Paul Ricoeur (1913–2005). Some key elements of the work of these two philosophers will be briefly considered below for the way in which it offers up a more sophisticated understanding of the role of language and interpretation for therapeutic practice.

Gadamer (1975/1996) and Ricoeur (1970, 1976, 1981) both emphasise the way in which language (or more properly, conversation and discourse) are the means by which we come to understand ourselves, others and the world more generally. That is, all meaning emerges through conversation as the world reveals itself to us phenomenologically. Like Heidegger, Gadamer (ibid.) believes that understanding is the key to existence and, like the later Heidegger, he stresses how this must come about through language, and in particular conversation. This does not mean that existence can or should be reduced to language but rather that all interpretive understanding necessarily comes about through forms of language. Gadamer argued that our understanding emerges out of *tradition* (our history and culture), with its own particular set of *prejudices* (limits to our way of perceiving the world). In order to recover meaning it is, therefore, necessary to engage with hermeneutics of meaning-recollection, methods designed to enable us to better understand the things in their appearing. Our understanding is both enabled and limited by our pre-understanding (our history, our culture: our worldview), the *horizons* of our way of understanding the world as it appears to us. There is always cultural distance and historical alienation when we try to understand, but we can and do gain mutual understanding through a *fusion of horizons*, a coming together or overlap between different world views. Therapy is very much engaged in this project as two people (or more) come together, each bound up by their *effective history* but committed to understand each other. The aim is a fusion of horizons through conversation to enable us to bridge the inevitable gap that exists between us, setting aside our pre-judgements as much as is possible through the phenomenological method, as we work to perceive the things in their appearing for our clients.

Ricoeur's work is vast and moves beyond Gadamer in some important ways, but his central project was to elaborate an understanding of the interpretation of text, a classic hermeneutic project. He went further than this, however, to discuss human action, narrative, ethics and politics. Like Gadamer, Ricoeur's work provides a theoretical position that recognises the embodied being-in-the-world of human beings that is beyond and pre-exists language, alongside an interpretive understanding of human nature through language. There are two ideas in Ricoeur's hermeneutic phenomenology that in my view are particularly important for therapists: his distinction between hermeneutics of empathy and suspicion and his work on narrative, particularly the way in which our identities are constructed through the stories we tell. Some of my own work has been focussed on bringing the ideas of Ricoeur to bear on both therapeutic practice and also research in such a way that we can more readily attend to language, power and politics (Langdridge, 2004, 2005b, 2007a, 2007b, 2008).

Ricoeur (1970) argues that all interpretation of meaning requires two elements: a *demythologising (empathic) hermeneutic* and a *demystifying (suspicious) hermeneutic*. The hermeneutics of empathy are the usual stuff of phenomenology, where we seek to understand the things in their appearing through a fusion of horizons. This is the interpretive process described by Heidegger and Gadamer that has formed the basis of much of this book. The second element is, however, much more controversial and, for some, anathema to phenomenology. Ricoeur argues that for full understanding more is needed than just the hermeneutics of empathy and that in addition it is necessary to employ hermeneutics of suspicion that enable us to identify meaning hidden beneath the surface. To this end, he explores the use of ideas from what he terms the 'three masters of suspicion': Freud, Marx and Nietzsche. With all three of these thinkers 'meaning' is in need of unmasking, whether this be through uncovering unconscious motivation (Freud), economic modes of production (Marx) or the will to power (Nietzsche). Ricoeur believed that these three thinkers demonstrated the inadequacy of gaining understanding through immediate consciousness alone (a hermeneutics of empathy), the project of phenomenology. I think Ricoeur raised an important issue for phenomenology though was misguided in his belief that the 'three masters' provided the solution. There is much that is not available to consciousness, with elements of our experience in darkness, not buried in some dynamic unconscious but rather not directly or immediately available to consciousness. If our actions were always simply explainable in terms of consciousness, then many of the problems that people encounter, and bring with them to therapy, would not arise at all. For me, therefore, there is potential in bringing some notion of suspicion into the therapeutic encounter. However, I argue that it is vital to re-think the hermeneutics of suspicion beyond Ricoeur if we are not simply going to import a method of interpretation that fundamentally undermines the phenomenology that is at the heart of the existential method.

I have built on Ricoeur's ideas about the use of hermeneutics to gain fuller understanding and propose a further distinction for hermeneutics of suspicion, between *depth hermeneutics* and *imaginative hermeneutics* (Langdridge, 2007a, 2007b). Depth hermeneutics are those methods of interpretation that require us to dig beneath the surface for hidden meaning, as we see employed in psychoanalysis. This form of hermeneutic is fundamentally at odds with the principles of phenomenological engagement, as it leads to a privileging of the analyst/therapist over the analysand/client. It undermines the phenomenology of the client, their lived experience, with their views subjugated to those of the therapist. Imaginative hermeneutics of suspicion are, by contrast, a way of moving beyond the apparent through a critical engagement with social theory. There is no digging beneath the surface but rather an exercise in imaginative play, augmented by specific social theoretical hermeneutics (such as those from feminism, critical race theory, queer theory), in order to enable the therapist and client to perceive their experiences differently. The aim is to be critical of the social world into which both client and therapist are thrown for the ways in which it both allows and limits how they can understand their experience. The aim is a *perspectival shift* in understanding such that new possibilities are opened up for how a client might understand their experience. This is particularly relevant for clients whose experience is inflected by oppression, such as those from sexual, gender, and racial minorities.

To give just one example of the need for a perspectival shift in understanding, which is followed up in detail below, involves that of lesbian and gay history. The early history of lesbian and gay social movements, that struggled against the tide of oppression only a relatively few years ago, demonstrates how important socio-cultural understandings are for our understanding of self and others. Lesbian and gay men came together to offer each other support in large cities and began to organise themselves to challenge the oppression that they faced in the 1960s. Like all new social movements this first entailed a process of consciousness raising, a process in which lesbian and gay people begin to recognise that they are not sick or evil. This is not as simple as it sounds when the social world into which people from oppressed minorities are thrown is one in which their sexual preferences are pathologised and criminalised. Psychiatrists would be invited to early lesbian and gay support/activist groups to explain how they were not evil but rather mentally ill. This was accepted and embraced as an example of a progressive shift in how lesbians and gay men could understand themselves. It was only later that people began to criticise this relatively new understanding and develop a sense of pride, based on a political story of equality, that such views were abandoned by lesbians and gay men themselves. These perspectival shifts in understanding occur at the intersection of individual and society, and the power of the social world into which we are thrown should never be underestimated.

My argument is that there is a place for imaginative hermeneutics of suspicion in therapy when working with clients from oppressed minorities, as a way of working with them in full acknowledgement of the impact of the social world on how they can understand themselves. Such hermeneutics would be those that are grounded in critical social theory designed to challenge oppression and offer up a different way of understanding the social world. This is a radical move for existential therapy, and one that does not abandon the client to their own fate within a politically naïve phenomenology but rather recognises the power of the therapist to work with clients in recognition of the way the social world limits possible ways of understanding. Whether the lines of oppression concern sexuality, gender, race or some other aspect of experience, there is the opportunity to bring the political into the therapy room in an explicit way rather than deny its inevitable presence and hide behind the mask of phenomenological impartiality.

How such hermeneutics are incorporated into practice is a complex and subtle affair, requiring considerable care that the political does not undermine the fundamentals of effective existential practice. It requires that we listen carefully to our client, aware of the limitations imposed by their perception of the social world, and then gently work with them to look at opening up possibilities, alternative ways that they might understand and speak about their experience. This is not about preaching to our clients or losing sight of their experience, but rather working with them gently to acknowledge the limits of their world view whilst pushing the boundaries of what they feel is available to them. At times this may involve us in concrete discussions of the broader social world along with our understanding of how this might influence us, but more often than not it will entail support for those moments when clients feel able to talk of themselves in a positive manner and gentle challenges when they do not.

Case study   Brian's search for his dream

Brian is 60 years old and came to see me about his difficulties dealing with his current relationship. He found me via the Internet where I am listed as a specialist in working with sexual and gender minority clients. He told me immediately about how he had visited two other therapists who thought he had a 'sex addiction problem' and that they could help him with this. He didn't think he had an addiction problem but said 'I guess if you say that too I'll have to believe it'. Internally I shuddered with horror at the thought that his experience had been subjugated to the particular theoretical bias of the therapist. I reassured him that I was interested in his own thoughts and feelings about his sexuality and that I also do not work with diagnostic categories around sex and sexuality. He then proceeded to tell me his story. His current difficulty concerned a sadomasochistic relationship he was struggling with in which he and his mistress were in conflict. She was based overseas and he had tried to live with her, but everything fell apart at this point. His dreams of a life as a slave were in tatters and he needed support from someone who would not judge him for his life choices. We worked together for some years with many ups and downs, as he attempted more than once to reconcile with his mistress. Every time he felt he was ready for this but then found it all failed again and again. What became clear was how his story was a simple one of a man and woman in love but unable to live with each other, unable to find a way to make the relationship work on a day-to-day level. Because he had found his dream he was unable to give this up and became increasingly distressed by the situation. This case highlighted for me the dangers of therapists failing to attend to the experience of a client from a phenomenological standpoint, with them seduced by pathologising theories of sexual addiction, alongside the need to recognise the broader social world in which we are all immersed. BDSM (bondage, dominance, submission, sadism and masochism) is still much misunderstood and is frequently pathologised rather than being seen for part of the variety of sexual behaviours and identities that a person may engage with. Brian's history spoke directly to such stories of pathology, in part due to his age and his own personal struggle to understand his own desires. It would have been all too easy to pick up those elements of his story of his own discomfort with his sexuality and see that as grounds for helping to 'cure him' of his 'problem', but that would have missed the point entirely. His problems were the result of the wider stigmatising social world into which he was thrown, and part of my role was in working with him to recognise societal prejudice and locate the real cause of his problems. They were not in his identity as a slave per se but rather a result of his difficulties in coming to terms with being part of a sexual minority, and also the very mundane reality of managing a relationship of any kind. We had considerable success in achieving a sense of contentment concerning his own understanding of his sexual identity, though struggled much more with coming to terms with the difficult reality of this one particular relationship. He thought he had found his dream, and that late in life this would never be possible again. He clung on to his failed relationship with dogged determination, refusing to give up on his dream, in spite of how much this hurt him. By drawing on hermeneutics critical of the pathologisation of sex and sexualities, I maintained a phenomenological stance that not only respected his experience but also worked to enable us both to locate his experience within a broader socio-cultural context in which BDSM is unfortunately still pathologised. That is, I worked actively with Brian such that we were both explicitly critical of the socio-cultural status quo, rather than expecting him to work against this on his own, and through this acknowledged the inevitably political quality of the therapeutic process. My experience with Brian moved me deeply; I was so impressed by his courage and determination to live his life to the full in the face of a social world that still so often fails to acknowledge and value difference.

Language – the power of narrative

The other element of Ricoeur's philosophy that speaks directly to our work as existential therapists concerns some of his later writing about narrative. Ricoeur (1984, 1985, 1988, 1992) moves away from classical hermeneutics to narrative as a result of his belief that it is through narratives that we can come to grasp the creation of new meaning fundamental to the human project. Many authors have written about the way in which we need to understand the stories people tell in order to understand human nature:

> If you want to know me, then you must know my story, for my story defines who I am. And if I want to know myself, to gain insight into the meaning of my own life, then I too must come to know my own story. (McAdams, 1993: 22)

Ricoeur (ibid.) argues that stories are constructed to make sense of our lived experience through the organisation of disparate elements into a meaningful whole. His argument is based on his understanding of time and his critical distinction between *cosmological time, phenomenological time* and *historical time*. Cosmological time refers to the effectively infinite nature of time associated with the cosmos. When we hear about the cosmos, our own experience of living in time is dwarfed through the enormity of scale and unintelligible nature of cosmic time. Phenomenological time, by contrast, is our everyday experience of time, lived through our finite and, relatively speaking, very short existence. We are bounded by the knowledge of our death and therefore acutely aware of our limited time on the earth. Historical time is an attempt to bridge the gap between our finite experience of time and the infinite nature of cosmic time, an attempt to reconcile the irreconcilable. Historical time achieves this through the inscription of existence on the cosmos by the production of *traces*, such as calenders, documents, historical records. These traces call for *emplotment* and the creation of narratives that transcend generations and enable us to make sense of the traces we have left on the planet.

At an individual human level, narratives enable us to situate our experience in phenomenological time. We are able to make sense of the individual episodes of our experience through their re-figuration, where we creatively transform individual episodes into a meaningful whole. Through the stories we construct we build a sense of who we are as our stories produce our narrative identities. If we want to know someone, we ask for their story and through understanding a person's story we come to understand them as a person. Identities are not therefore fixed but instead contingent, historically and culturally specific and unique to each individual. All therapy involves us beginning by asking for our client to tell their story as it relates to their presenting concern. The nature of the story they tell is revealing. So many clients are stuck with a story of selfhood in which past episodes become fixed, sedimented into their present story, and with this their future determined in ways that are problematic. The emotional tone and narrative identity being conjured up in a client's story offer us insights into their lifeworld and yet more clues for how we might work with them better (see the case study below). The project of existential therapy is, therefore, hermeneutic with us seeking to understand the other in conversation through the stories they tell such that we are able to help them find better ways of storying their lives that open up rather than close down future possibilities.

Case study   Andrew's lightness of being

Andrew came to see me as he felt he was not as engaged with life as he wanted to be. He had recently separated from a long-term partner and was worried that he didn't seem to care enough about life and what it meant to him. When he attended for his first session he breezed through his story barely stopping for breath. He covered so much and yet stayed with so little. His story included the death of his sister, his coming-out, moving country and family difficulties. The story was coherent and considered but the emotional tone was light throughout. Andrew spoke about getting little support from his friends and family concerning the recent relationship break up, and I decided to make a somewhat challenging intervention about his own role in this. I spoke of how nothing appeared to be a problem for him and that my experience of him was of someone who just breezed through life. This stopped him in his tracks as he paused for thought before moving on swiftly. My intervention came from my own sense about his narrative identity, conjured up through the way he storied the episodes in his life (the process of emplotment). For some, a story containing these episodes may have been tragic or heartfelt, but not with Andrew. Instead, I witnessed a lightness of being that, to me, spoke to the heart of his presenting problems. This intervention and my thoughts about Andrew were still just possibilities, and the next few sessions focussed on us exploring his lifeworld in more detail. As he revealed the manifold of his experience I began to see how Andrew felt the need to take ultimate responsibility for his own life, perhaps at the expense of allowing others to support him, whilst deep down he craved such support and felt aggrieved when others (such as his former partner) received it. He constructed his identity as someone who was going somewhere, who needed to succeed and achieve, almost entirely future focussed, and there was little room to stop and contemplate his present or past. Failure was not an option, in anything he did, resulting in his breezy lightness of being. Our work centred on staying with his present and allowing space for discussion of his past, with me working actively to help him re-figure the episodes of his life into a new narrative identity that enabled him to both maintain his positive future focus and not lose sight of the meaning of events in the present or past. The focus on the way in which experience is recounted through the stories we tell of ourselves was particularly fruitful in this case. We honed in on key moments for him and in particular his relationships with others, thinking through their meaning in the stories he told. We also looked explicitly at his identity (conjured up through the way he spoke of the episodes of his life) and what he gained and lost by speaking of himself as he did now. Much of this involved me bringing my own experience of him into the therapy room. This enabled Andrew to see that he could speak of his experience differently (and, therefore, re-figure the episodes of his life such that a new narrative identity emerged), should he wish, and with some experimentation find a new way of being that not only looked to the future but also allowed space for the present, inflected by the past.

Language is clearly central to existential therapy – it is after all one of the 'talking therapies' – but there is much more to language than it being simply the medium/tool by which we express what we think and feel to ourselves and others. A number of philosophers, within and outside the existential tradition, have offered up important challenges to any simple representational notion of language. Perhaps the most significant philosophical development in recent years has been the rise of postmodernism and the consequent turn to discourse, or perhaps more accurately, text. Postmodernism concerns a rejection of the 'grand narratives' of the enlightenment, notably the notion of progressive knowledge, increasing understanding and emancipation through truth (Lyotard, 1979/2004). One additional significant consequence of postmodern thinking in philosophy is a turn to discourse, a focus on the way in which all understanding emerges through language. The thought of philosophers such as Foucault, Derrida, Deleuze and others is particularly influential here and their work has been taken up by many people within the human sciences, including many counsellors and psychotherapists. The thought of such philosophers is radically different from that of the existentialists (or indeed, the hermeneuticists) and offers a critical challenge for those of us working within a broadly phenomenological framework. With such philosophies we see a questioning of the taken-for-granted assumption that language is a transparent medium in which a speaker is simply able to communicate their experience to a listener. What these philosophers have argued is that language is much more complex than this, having a functional component as well as a semantic component, and even more challenging still that there is nothing beyond language itself. That is, since meaning can only be communicated through language, then it is language itself that allows and limits all understanding. There is undoubtedly some truth in these arguments, though such claims have often been overstated, and there is a need for existential therapists to take some of the concerns raised more seriously than they do at present. Existential and hermeneutic philosophers have, of course, considered the role of language and the way in which meanings are communicated through language, as outlined above. Heidegger (1927/1962) himself raised the issue of language – or rather discourse – recognising the way in which it is discourse that is the medium by which shared understanding comes about. Later still, Heidegger (1947/1993: 217) refers to 'language as the house of being' and further elaborates how language is not simply a tool for communicating meaning but fundamental in revealing the world and our relationship to it. It is Ricoeur, however, and his turn to narrative who is, in my view, the most important thinker on this subject for existential therapists. His turn to narrative was instructive, for whilst there is recognition of the complexity of language, and a need to work harder to appreciate this complexity, there remains a speaking subject and reference to the shared lifeworld that we all inhabit and not a slide to the textual or linguistic reductionism that we see with many postmodern writers. There is much more work to be done to fully realise the implications of these ideas in practice, but doing so is key to keeping existential therapy a vital force within the shifting terrain of contemporary developments in counselling and psychotherapy.

The future of existential therapy

Existential therapy is clearly a somewhat marginal approach to counselling and psychotherapy. It does not have the popularity or wider acknowledgement of person-centred counselling or psychoanalysis, nor the institutional recognition of cognitive behavioural therapy. It does, however, have a proud history and there are signs of growth both in the numbers of people training and practising as existential therapists and those interested in ideas from existential philosophy from other therapeutic perspectives. In the UK in particular there are two major training centres for existential therapy (the New School of Psychotherapy and Counselling and Regent's College), both of which offer professional trainings in existential counselling and psychotherapy. The Society for Existential Analysis also provides a professional network for people interested in both theory and practice and the Society journal, *Existential Analysis* (edited by Simon du Plock and Greg Madison), is clearly going from strength to strength. Beyond the UK there are centres for existential therapy in many European countries, the Americas, the Indo-Pacific region and beyond. Outside the UK there are also many academic and professional journals that publish work concerning, or of relevance to, existential therapy including, for instance, the *International Journal of Existential Psychology and Psychotherapy*, the *Journal of Phenomenological Psychology*, the *Indo-Pacific Journal of Phenomenology*, the *Journal of Humanistic Psychology* and *The Humanistic Psychologist*. The International Human Sciences Research Conference is now in its 30th year and provides a truly international forum for discussion and debate on a wide variety of issues in the human sciences, including existential psychotherapy, alongside other smaller conferences such as those organised by the Society for Existential Analysis, amongst others.

There are some challenges for existential counselling and psychotherapy which we fail to address at our peril. First, there is the challenge of building a strong research tradition within the field. This already exists within academic phenomenological psychology (see Langdridge, 2007b), but there is still much to do to put existential therapy on a more or less equal footing with other therapeutic modalities. Individual therapists, as well as those of us within wider academic and professional networks, can contribute here. It is vital that we all engage with research more fully and contribute knowledge about theory and practice to academic and professional journals. The growth of discourses around evidence-based practice provide a real challenge for existential therapy if it is to occupy a place alongside other forms of therapy within professional settings. Second, there is a need for continued work to develop theory to inform practice. There is a tendency amongst some, though by no means all, existential therapists to simply return to well-trodden theoretical ground and ignore contemporary developments in theory and practice, let alone contribute to them. Whilst we must never lose sight of the core of existential counselling and psychotherapy, this does not mean that we should not work to move ideas forward. A word of warning is in order here, however. This does not mean that we should be looking for the latest idea or development to add on to or replace existing practice. Newer is not necessarily better, nor is an eclectic approach to therapy, and there are many fads in the world of therapy which offer little that actually improves our practice and the work we do with our clients. With continued efforts to conduct more research, develop theory and engage with the contemporary challenges that we all must face, existential therapy should have an assured future.

Further reading

Ricoeur, P. (1970). *Freud and philosophy: an essay on interpretation* (trans D. Savage). New Haven, NJ: Yale University Press.
   Arguably Ricoeur's most important work, where he provides his critical challenge to phenomenology through his analysis of Freud.

Ricoeur, P. (1976). *Interpretation theory: discourse and the surplus of meaning.* Forth Worth, TX: Texas Christian University Press.
   One of the more accessible pieces of writing by Ricoeur and a good introduction to some of his thoughts.

Ricoeur, P. (1981). *Hermeneutics and the human sciences* (Ed. and trans. J. B. Thompson). Cambridge: Cambridge University Press.
   Another reasonably accessible selection of Ricoeur's writing and one of the most relevant for psychology and the social sciences more generally.

Samuels, A. (1993). *The political psyche.* London: Routledge.
   A powerful book highlighting the need for serious consideration of the relationship between psychotherapy and politics.

References

Adams, M. (2001). Practising phenomenology – some reflections and considerations. *Existential Analysis, 12*(1), 65–84.

American Psychiatric Association (2000). *Diagnostic and statistical manual of the American Psychiatric Association* (DSM-IV TR). Arlington, VA: APA.

Anderson, K. & Cissna, K. N. (1997). *The Martin Buber–Carl Rogers dialogue: a new transcript and commentary*. Albany, NY: SUNY Press.

Asay, T. P. & Lambert, M. J. (1999). The empirical case for the common factors in therapy: quantitative findings. In M. Hubble, B. L. Duncan & S. D. Miller (Eds), *The heart and soul of change: what works in therapy* (pp. 33–55). Washington, DC: American Psychological Association.

Ashworth, P. (2003a). The phenomenology of the lifeworld and social psychology. *Social Psychological Review, 5*(1), 18–34.

Ashworth, P. (Ed.) (2003b). An approach to phenomenological psychology: the contingencies of the lifeworld. *Journal of Phenomenological Psychology, 34*(2), 145–156.

Ashworth, P. & Cheung Chung, M. (Eds) (2006). *Phenomenology and psychological science*. New York: Springer.

Barkham, M. (2003). Quantitative research on psychotherapeutic interventions: methods and findings across four research generations. In R. Woolfe, W. Dryden & S. Strawbridge (Eds), *Handbook of counselling psychology* (pp. 25–73). London: Sage.

Barkham, M. & Barker, M. (2003). Outcome research. In M. Barker, A. Vossler & D. Langdridge (Eds), *Understanding counselling and psychotherapy*. London: Sage.

Baumeister, R. F. (1991). *Meanings of life*. New York: Guilford Press.

Becker, E. (1973). *The denial of death*. New York: Free Press Paperbacks.

Bell, D. (1990). *Husserl*. London: Routledge.

Berk, R. A. & Rossi, P. H. (1990). *Thinking about program evaluation*. Newbury Park, CA: Sage.

Binswanger, L. (1958). The existential analysis school of thought. In R. May, E. Angel & H. F. Ellenberger (Eds), *Existence*. New York: Basic Books.

Binswanger, L. (1963). *Being in the world* (trans. J. Needleman). New York: Basic Books.

Bohart, A. C. & Tallman, K. (1999). *How clients make therapy work: the process of active self-healing*. Washington, DC: American Psychological Association.

Bond, T. (2009). *Standards and ethics for counselling in action* (3rd edn). London: Sage.

Boss, M. (1957). *The analysis of dreams* (trans. A. J. Pomerans). London: Rider.

Boss, M. (1963). *Psychoanalysis and daseinsanalysis*. New York: Basic Books.

Bowers, L. (1998). *The social nature of mental illness*. London: Routledge.

Buber, M. (1923/1958). *I and thou*. Edinburgh: T. and T. Clark.

Cohn, H. (1997). *Existential thought and therapeutic practice: an introduction to existential psychotherapy*. London: Sage.

Cohn, H. (2002). *Heidegger and the roots of existential therapy*. London: Continuum.

Cooper, D. E. (1999). *Existentialism* (2nd edn). Oxford: Blackwell.

Cooper, M. (2003). *Existential therapies*. London: Sage.

Cooper, M. (2004a). Viagra for the brain: psychotherapy research and the challenge to existential therapeutic practice. *Existential Analysis, 15*(1), 2–14.

Cooper, M. (2004b). Encountering self-otherness: I–I and I–Me modes of self-relating. In H. J. M. Hermans & G. Dimaggio (Eds), *Dialogical self in psychotherapy* (pp. 60–73). Hove: Bruner-Routledge.

Cooper, M. (2008). *Essential research findings in counselling and psychotherapy: the facts are friendly*. London: Sage.

Cooper, M. & Adams, M. (2005). Death. In E. van Deurzen & C. Arnold-Baker (Eds), *Existential perspectives on human issues* (pp. 78–85). Palgrave Macmillan: Basingstoke.

Dahlberg, K., Dahlberg, H. & Nyström, M. (2008). *Reflective lifeworld research*. Lund: Studentlitteratur.

De Beauvoir, S. (1947/1976). *The ethics of ambiguity* (trans. B. Frechtman). New York: Kensington.

De Beauvoir, S. (1949/1972). *The second sex* (trans. H. Parshley). Harmondsworth: Penguin.

Deurzen, E. van (1996). Existential therapy. In W. Dryden (Ed.) *Handbook of individual therapy*. London: Sage.

Deurzen, E. van (1998). *Paradox and passion in psychotherapy*. Chichester: Wiley.

Deurzen, E. van (2002). *Existential counselling and psychotherapy in practice* (2nd edn). London: Sage.

Deurzen, E. van (2009). *Psychotherapy and the quest for happiness*. London: Sage.

Deurzen, E. van & Adams, M. (2011). *Skills in existential counselling & psychotherapy*. London: Sage.

Deurzen-Smith, E. van (1984). Existential psychotherapy. In W. Dryden (Ed.), *Individual therapy in Britain*. London: Harper and Row.

Deurzen-Smith, E. van (1988). *Existential counselling in practice*. London: Sage.

Deurzen-Smith, E. van (1997). *Everyday mysteries: existential dimensions of psychotherapy*. London: Routledge.

Descartes, R. (1641/2003). *Meditations on first philosophy* (trans. D. M. Clarke). London: Penguin.

Doyle, (2001). Nietzsche's justification of the will to power. *Pli: The Warwick Journal of Philosophy, 11*, 79–102.

Dreyfus, H. L. (2009). The roots of existentialism. In H. L. Dreyfus & M. A. Wrathall (Eds), *A companion to phenomenology and existentialism*. Oxford: Wiley-Blackwell.

Dreyfus, H. L. & Wrathall, M. A. (2009). *A companion to phenomenology and existentialism*. Chichester: Wiley-Blackwell.

Elliott, R. (2002). Hermeneutic single-case efficacy design. *Psychotherapy Research*, I(1), 1–21.

Farber, L. H. (2000). O death, where is thy sting-a-ling-ling? In R. Boyers & A. Farber (Eds), *The ways of the will: selected essays* (pp. 247–272). New York: Basic Books.

Fell, J. P. (1965). *Emotion in the thought of Sartre*. New York: Columbia University Press.

Finlay, L. (2011). *Phenomenology for therapists*. Chichester: Wiley-Blackwell.

Finlay, L. & Evans, K. (2009). *Relational-centred research for psychotherapists: exploring meanings and experience*. Chichester: Wiley-Blackwell.

Firestone, R. W. (1994). Psychological defenses against death anxieties. In R. A. Neimeyer (Ed.), *Death anxiety handbook: research, instrumentation and application* (pp. 217–241). New York: Taylor & Francis.

Freud, S. (1900). The interpretation of dreams. In J. Strachey (Ed.), (1953). *The standard edition of the complete psychological works of Sigmund Freud* (vol. IV). London: Vintage, Hogarth Press and the Institute of Psycho-Analysis.

Freud, S. (1901/1979). The case of Dora. *Pelican Freud Library* (vol. 8: Case Histories I). Harmondsworth: Penguin.

Freud, S. (1909/1979). Notes upon a case of obsessional neurosis (the 'rat man'). *Pelican Freud Library* (vol. 9: Case Histories II). Harmondsworth: Penguin.

Gadamer, H. (1975/1996). *Truth and method*. London: Sheed and Ward.

Giorgi, A. (2009). *The descriptive phenomenological method in psychology: a modified Husserlian approach*. Pittsburgh, PA: Duquesne University Press.

Grant, M. (Ed.) (2000). *The Raymond Tallis reader*. Basingstoke: Palgrave Macmillan.

Greenberg, J., Koole, S. L. & Pyszczynski, T. (Eds) (2004). *Handbook of experimental existential psychology*. New York: Guilford Press.

Grosz, E. (1994). *Volatile bodies: toward a corporeal feminism*. Bloomington: Indiana University Press.

Halling, S. & Dearborn Nill, J. (1995). A brief history of existential-phenomenological psychiatry and psychotherapy. *Journal of Phenomenological Psychology, 26*(1), 1–45.

Heidegger, M. (1927/1962). *Being and time*. (1962 text trans. J. Macquarrie & E. Robinson). Oxford: Blackwell.

Heidegger, M. (1947/1993). Letter on humanism. In M. Heidegger, *Basic writings* (edited by D. F. Krell). London: Routledge.

Heidegger, M. (1982). The basic problem of phenomenology (trans. A. Hofstadter). Bloomington: Indiana University Press.

Heidegger, M. (1987/2001). *Zollikon seminars: protocols – conversations – letters* (trans. F. Mayr & R. Askay). Evanston, IL: Northwestern University Press.

Hoeller, K. (1999). Introduction. *Review of Existential Psychology and Psychiatry, 24*, v–viii.

Husserl, E. (1900–01/1970). *Logical investigations* (2 vols) (trans. J. N. Findlay). New York: Humanities Press.

Husserl, E. (1913/1931). *Ideas: a general introduction to pure phenomenology* (trans. W. R. Boyce Gibson). London: Allen & Unwin.

Husserl, E. (1936/1970). *The crisis of European sciences and transcendental philosophy* (trans. D. Carr). Evanston, IL: Northwestern University Press.

Ihde, D. (1986). *Experimental phenomenology: an introduction.* Albany, NY: SUNY Press.

Isay, R. A. (1989). *Being homosexual: gay men and their development.* New York: Avon Books.

Jaenicke, U. (1996). Dream interpretation, the 'royal road' to the dreamer's actual and existential suffering and striving. *Journal of the Society for Existential Analysis, 8*(1), 105–114.

Jaspers, K. (1932/1971). *Philosophy of existence* (trans. R. F. Grabay). Philadelphia, PA: University of Pennsylvania Press. (Originally published 1932 as *Existenzphilosophie*.)

Kagen, N. (1984). Interpersonal process recall: basic methods and recent research. In D. Larson (Ed.), *Teaching psychological skills: models for giving psychology away* (pp. 229–244). Monterey, CA: Brooks/Cole.

Kaufmann, W. (1983). Bubers fehlschläge und sein triumph. In J. Bloch and G. Hayyim (Eds), *Martin Buber. bilanz seines denkens* (pp. 22ff). Freiburg im Breisgau: Herder.

Kierkegaard, S. (1843a/1992). *Either/or* (trans. A. Hannay, ed. V. Eremita). London: Penguin.

Kierkegaard, S. (1843b/1985). *Fear and trembling* (trans. A. Hannay). London: Penguin.

Krupnik, J. L., Sotsky, S. M., Simmens, S., Moyer, J., Elkin, I., Watkins, J. & Pilkonis, P. A. (1996). The role of the therapeutic alliance in psychotherapy and pharmacotherapy outcome: findings from the National Institute of Mental Health treatment of depression collaborative research programme. *Journal of Consulting and Clinical Psychology, 64*(3), 532–539.

Laing, R. D. (1960). *The divided self.* Harmondsworth: Penguin.

Laing, R. D. (1961). *Self and others.* Harmondsworth: Penguin.

Laing, R. D. (1967). *The politics of experience.* Harmondsworth: Penguin.

Langdridge, D. (2004). The hermeneutic phenomenology of Paul Ricoeur: problems and possibilities for existential-phenomenological psychotherapy. *Existential Analysis, 15*(2), 243–255.

Langdridge, D. (2005a). 'The child's relations with others': Merleau-Ponty, embodiment and psychotherapy. *Existential Analysis*, *16*(1), 87–99.

Langdridge, D. (2005b). Between ideology and utopia: re-thinking conflict and reconciliation in psychotherapy. *Existential Analysis*, *16*(2), 221–235.

Langdridge, D. (2006). Imaginative variations on selfhood: elaborating an existential-phenomenological approach to dream analysis. *Existential Analysis*, *17*(1), 2–13.

Langdridge, D. (2007a). Gay affirmative therapy: a theoretical framework and defence. *Journal of Gay and Lesbian Psychotherapy*, *11*(1), 27–43.

Langdridge, D. (2007b). *Phenomenological psychology: theory, research and method*. Harlow: Pearson Education.

Langdridge, D. (2008) Phenomenology and critical social psychology: directions and debates in theory and research. *Social and Personality Psychology Compass*, *2*(3), 1126–1142 (DOI: 10.1111/j.1751-9004.2008.00114.x).

Langdridge, D. (2009). Relating through difference: a critical narrative analysis. In L. Finlay & K. Evans (Eds), *Relational centred research for psychotherapists: exploring meanings and experience* (pp. 213–226). Chichester: Wiley-Blackwell.

Langdridge, D. (2010). Existential psychotherapy. In M. Barker, A. Vossler & D. Langdridge (Eds), *Understanding counselling and psychotherapy*. London: Sage.

Langdridge, D. & Barker, M. (Eds) (2007). *Safe, sane and consensual: contemporary perspectives on sadomasochism*. Basingstoke: Palgrave Macmillan.

Langdridge, D. & Hagger-Johnson, G. (2009). *Introduction to research methods and data analysis in psychology* (2nd edn). Harlow: Pearson Education.

Langer, M. (1989). *Merleau-Ponty's phenomenology of perception: a guide and commentary*. Basingstoke: Macmillan.

Le Doeuff, M. (1991). *Hipparchia's choice: an essay concerning women, philosophy etc.* (trans. T. Selous). Oxford: Blackwell.

Levinas, E. (1961/1987). *Totality and infinity* (trans. A. Lingis). Pittsburgh, PA: Duquesne University Press.

Levinas, E. (1974/1981). *Otherwise than being, or beyond essence* (trans. A. Lingis). Kluwer: Martinus Nijhoff.

Lewis, M. (1993). Emergence of human emotions. In M. Lewis & J. M. Haviland (Eds), *Handbook of emotions*. London: Guilford Press.

Lyotard, J.-F. (1979/2004). *The postmodern condition: a report on knowledge* (trans. G. Bennington & B. Massumi). Manchester: Manchester University Press.

MacDonald, P. S. (2001). Husserl's preemptive responses to existentialist critiques. *Indo-Pacific Journal of Phenomenology*, *1*(1), April, available to download from www.ipjp.org.

Macquarrie, J. (1986). *Existentialism: an introduction, guide and assessment.* Harmondsworth: Penguin.

Mahrer, A. R., Nadler, W. P., Dessaulles, A., Gervaize, P. A. & Sterner, I. (1987). Good and very good moments in psychotherapy: content, distribution and facilitation. *Psychotherapy, 24,* 7–14.

Maluccio, A. N. (1979). *Learning from clients: interpersonal helping as viewed by clients and social workers.* New York: Macmillan.

Malyon, A. K. (1982). Psychotherapeutic implications of internalised homophobia in gay men. In J. C. Gonsiorek (Ed.), *Homosexuality and psychotherapy: a practitioner's handbook of affirmative models* (pp. 59–69). Binghamton, NY: Haworth Press.

May, R. (1983). *The discovery of being.* New York: W. W. Norton.

May, R. (1999). Existential psychology and the problem of death. *Review of Existential Psychology and Psychiatry, 24,* 40–48.

May, R., Angel, E. & Ellenberger, H.F. (1958). *Existence.* New York: Basic Books.

McAdams, D. (1993). *The stories we live by: personal myths and the making of the self.* New York: Guilford Press.

McLeod, J. (2003). *Doing counselling research.* London: Sage.

Mearns, D. & Cooper, M. (2005). *Working at relational depth in counselling and psychotherapy.* London: Sage.

Merleau-Ponty, M. (1945/1962). *Phenomenology of perception* (trans. C. Smith). London: Routledge.

Merleau-Ponty, M. (1964/1968). *The visible and the invisible* (trans. A. Lingis). Evanston, IL: Northwestern University Press.

Minkowski, E. (1933/1970). Lived time: phenomenological and psychopathological studies (trans. N. Mekell). Evanston, IL: Northwestern University Press.

Moran, D. (2000). *Introduction to phenomenology.* London: Routledge.

Morley, S. (1989). Single case research. In G. Parry and F. N. Watts (Eds), *Behavioural and mental health research: a handbook of skills and methods* (pp. 233–264). Hillsdale, NJ: Lawrence Erlbaum.

Nietzsche, F. (1882/1972). *The gay science* (trans. W. Kaufmann). New York: Random House.

Nietzsche, F. (1883–85/2003). *Thus spoke Zarathustra: a book for all and none* (trans. R. J. Hollindale). Harmondsworth: Penguin.

Nietzsche, F. (1908/1979). *Ecco Homo* (trans. W. Kaufman & R. J. Hollindale). New York: Vintage.

Peperzak, A. T., Critchley, S. & Bernasconi, R. (Eds.) (1996). *Emmanuel Levinas: basic philosophical writings.* Bloomington: Indiana University Press.

Polkinghorne, D. E. (1988). *Narrative knowing and the human sciences.* Albany, NY: SUNY Press.

Polt, R. (1999). *Heidegger: an introduction.* London: UCL Press.

Rennie, D. L. (1990). Toward a representation of the client's experience of the psychotherapy hour. In S. G. Toukmanian & D. L. Rennie (Eds),

Psychotherapy process research: paradigmatic and narrative approaches (pp. 211–233). Newbury Park, CA: Sage.

Rennie, D. L. (2002). Experiencing psychotherapy: grounded theory studies. In D. J. Cain & J. Seeman (Eds), *Humanistic psychotherapies: handbook of research and practice* (pp. 117–144). Washington, DC: American Psychological Association.

Reynolds, J. (2006). *Understanding existentialism*. Stocksfield: Acumen.

Rice, L. N. & Greenberg, L. S. (Eds) (1984). *Patterns of change: intensive analysis of psychotherapy process*. New York: Guilford Press.

Ricoeur, P. (1970). *Freud and philosophy: an essay on interpretation* (trans. D. Savage). New Haven, CT: Yale University Press.

Ricoeur, P. (1976). *Interpretation theory: discourse and the surplus of meaning*. Forth Worth, TX: Texas Christian University Press.

Ricoeur, P. (1981). *Hermeneutics and the human sciences* (ed. and trans. J. B. Thompson). Paris: Edition de la Maison des Sciences de l'Homme/ Cambridge: Cambridge University Press.

Ricoeur, P. (1984). *Time and narrative* (vol. 1) (trans. K. McLaughlin & D. Pellauer). Chicago, IL: University of Chicago Press.

Ricoeur, P. (1985). *Time and narrative* (vol. 2) (trans. K. McLaughlin & D. Pellauer). Chicago, IL: University of Chicago Press.

Ricoeur, P. (1988). *Time and narrative* (vol. 3) (trans. K. McLaughlin & D. Pellauer). Chicago, IL: University of Chicago Press.

Ricoeur, P. (1992). *Oneself as another* (trans. K. Blamey). Chicago, IL: University of Chicago Press.

Ricoeur, P. (1996). *Lectures on ideology and utopia* (ed. G. H. Taylor). New York: Columbia University Press.

Ritter, K. Y. & Terndrup, A. I. (2002). *Handbook of affirmative psychotherapy with lesbians and gay men*. New York: Guilford Press.

Rogers, C. R. (1942). *Counselling and psychotherapy: newer concepts in practice*. Boston, MA: Houghton & Mifflin.

Rogers, C. R. (1951). *Client-centred therapy*. London: Constable.

Rogers, C. R. (1961). *On becoming a person: a therapist's view of therapy*. London: Constable.

Rogers, C. R. (1980). *A way of being*. Boston, MA: Houghton & Mifflin.

Rowland, N. & Goss, S. (Eds) (2000). *Evidence-based counselling and psychological therapies: research and applications*. London: Routledge.

Samuels, A. (1993). *The political psyche*. London: Routledge.

Sartre, J.-P. (1939/2002). *Sketch for a theory of the emotions* (trans. P. Mairet). London: Routledge.

Sartre, J.-P. (1943/1956). *Being and nothingness: an essay on phenomenological ontology* (trans. H. Barnes). New York: Philosophical Library.

Sartre, J.-P. (1943/2003). *Being and nothingness*. London: Routledge.

Sartre, J.-P. (1948/1995). *Anti-semite and Jew* (trans. G. J. Becker). New York: Schocken.

Sartre, J.-P. (1952/1964). *Saint Genet: actor and martyr* (trans. B. Frechtman). London: W. H. Allen.

Sartre, J.-P. (1960/2004). *Critique of dialectical reason* (trans. A. Sheridan-Smith). New York: Verso.

Sartre, J.-P. (1971). *The idiot of the family* (trans. C. Cosman). Chicago, IL: University of Chicago Press.

Shidlo, A. (1994). Internalized homophobia: conceptual and empirical issues in measurement. In B. Greene & G.M. Herek (Eds), *Lesbian and gay psychology: theory, research, and clinical applications* (pp. 176–205). Thousand Oaks, CA: Sage.

Smith, J. A., Flowers, P. & Larkin, M. (2009). *Interpretative phenomenological analysis: theory, method and research*. London: Sage.

Sokolowski, R. (2000). *Introduction to phenomenology*. Cambridge: Cambridge University Press.

Spaten, O. M., Byrialsen, M. N. & Langdridge, D. (in press). Men's grief, meaning and growth: a phenomenological investigation of the meaning of loss. *Indo-Pacific Journal of Phenomenology*.

Spinelli, E. (1996). Some hurried notes expressing outline ideas that someone might someday utilise as signposts towards a sketch of an existential-phenomenological theory of human sexuality. *Journal of the Society for Existential Analysis*, 8(1): 2–20.

Spinelli, E. (2006). *Demystifying therapy*. Ross-on-Wye: PCCS Books.

Spinelli, E. (2007). *Practising existential psychotherapy: the relational world*. London: Sage.

Strasser, F. (2005). *Emotions: experiences in existential psychotherapy and life*. London: Duckworth.

Szasz, T. (1961). *The myth of mental illness*. New York: Harper & Row.

Tantam, D. (2005). Groups. In E. van Deurzen & C. Arnold-Baker (Eds), *Existential perspectives on human issues* (pp. 143–154). Basingstoke: Palgrave.

Tillich, P. (1967). The eternal now. In N.A. Scott (Ed.), *The modern vision of death*. Richmond, VA: John Knox Press.

Todres, L. (2007). *Embodied enquiry: phenomenological touchstones for research, psychotherapy and spirituality*. Basingstoke: Palgrave.

Van Manen, M. (1990). *Researching lived experience: human science for an action sensitive pedagogy*. Albany, NY: SUNY Press.

Walsh, R. A. & McElwain, B. (2002). Existential psychotherapies. In D. J. Cain & J. Seeman (Eds), *Humanistic psychotherapy: handbook of research and practice*. Washington, DC: American Psychological Association.

Warnock, M. (1970). *Existentialism*. Oxford: Oxford University Press.

World Health Organisation (2004). *International classification of diseases* (ICD-10). Geneva: WHO.

Yalom, I. (1980). *Existential psychotherapy*. New York: Basic Books.

Yalom, I. (1989). *Love's executioner and other tales of psychotherapy*. New York: Basic Books.

Yalom, I. (2005). *When Nietzsche wept*. New York: Harper Collins.

Young, I. M. (1985). Pregnant subjectivity and the limits of existential phenomenology. In D. Ihde & H. J. Silverman (Eds), *Descriptions* (pp. 25–35). New York: SUNY Press.

Young, I. M. (1990). Throwing like a girl. In *Throwing like a girl and other essays in feminist philosophy and social theory*. Bloomington: Indiana University Press.

Zank, M. (2007). Martin Buber. In E. N. Zalta (Ed.), *The Stanford encyclopedia of philosophy* (Fall 2008 edn) (http://plato.stanford.edu/archives/fall2008/entries/buber/).

Index